I count my family extraordinarily blessed to have a wise and thoughtful pastor in Scott Patty. This devotional will show you why. This book will guide you, day-by-day, into a deeper sense of the love and holiness and presence of our God. Moving through these short meditations will take very little time from your day, but can change your life for the good in ways you might not expect.

**Russell Moore**, president of the Ethics and Religious Liberty Commission of the Southern Baptist Convention

Scott Patty is one of my heroes here in Nashville. He is a pastor with a keen mind, a tender heart, and wise instincts. If he were my pastor, I would be fortunate indeed. But now through *Words of Grace: A 100-Day Devotional*, Scott serves us all, leading us into the green pastures and beside the still waters of daily gospel refreshment. I hope you will pick up this book and join me there!

**Ray Ortlund**, pastor of Immanuel Church, Nashville, Tennessee, author of *The Gospel: How the Church Portrays the Beauty of Christ* and *Marriage and the Mystery of the Gospel*

None of us can live by bread alone, but only by every word that proceeds from the mouth of God. And we need this food every day. Scott Patty's *Words of Grace* sets before us bite-sized meals of truth from God's word that we can chew on throughout the day.

**Nancy Guthrie**, author of the *Seeing Jesus in the Old Testament* Bible study series

For several reasons, it's a great joy and honor to endorse Scott Patty's new book, *Words of Grace*. I've known Scott for over twenty-five years, and long before he wrote these "words of grace," he lived them before me, and extended them to me. As a fellow pastor and friend, I've had a ring-side seat, watching my brother's informed mind, enflamed heart, and extended hands express the gospel of God's grace in the greater Nashville community. Through the joys, pains, and transitions of life and ministry, Scott has been one of my main models of a leader smitten with the glory and grace of Jesus. Marinate in these 100 wonderful devotionals, and you'll see what I mean.

**Scotty Smith**, pastor emeritus of West End Community Church, Franklin and teacher in residence of West End Community Church, Nashville

Thank God He has not left us without a word. For it is by God's Word that we can know Him and know of His great promises through the gospel. *Words of Grace* will, I believe, serve as a catalyst for the people of God to again and again drink deeply from the Word of God and have their souls refreshed by our gracious God. It has been for me, and I pray it will be for you as well.

**Michael Kelley**, Director of Discipleship, LifeWay Christian Resources

Confusing times beg for clarity. In this book, Scott Patty gives readers fresh insight infused with timeless truth, saying more with fewer words. Whatever you're facing, this book offers clarity from the core of the Christian faith.

**John Kramp**, SVB and Bible Publisher, HarperCollins Christian Publishing

# WORDS

*of*

# GRACE

A 100-DAY

DEVOTIONAL

SCOTT PATTY

B&H
PUBLISHING GROUP

NASHVILLE, TENNESSEE

978-1-4627-7464-7

Published by B&H Publishing Group
Nashville, Tennessee

Dewey Decimal Classification: 242.5
Subject Heading: DEVOTIONAL LITERATURE / GRACE
(THEOLOGY) / FAITH

1 2 3 4 5 6 7 • 22 21 20 19 18

For Grace Community Church of Nashville

# Contents

# Section II: God's Work in Our Lives

# Section III: Responding to God in Faith

# Introduction

God has graciously given us the Bible. The Bible is the collection of God's words, given to his chosen men who wrote them under the inspiration of his Spirit (2 Tim. 3:16; 2 Pet. 1:20–21). Sometimes the Bible is called the Scripture, which means sacred writings. We also call the Bible the Word of God, because the words in the Bible make up the message of God to us about his great plan of salvation for sinful people.

In the Bible, God is communicating to us. He is speaking words of *grace*. That means he is showing us our need of him and calling us to come to him in faith. As a Christian and a pastor, I want people to hear God's Word, see the grace of Christ in it, respond to him in faith, and come to know him personally. That's why I preach from the Bible every Sunday, talk to people about the Bible in conversation, and write to explain passages of the Bible and how they relate to us.

The devotional writings included in this book were originally written for the congregation I have served for twenty-five years. They have been edited so readers who are not members of our church can benefit from them without the specific details of our congregation and city.

I call these devotional writings *Words of Grace* because they are designed to open up the meaning, relevance, and application of God's Word of grace to people. As you read them you will notice several things.

First, these devotionals are based on Bible passages. When I write, it is God's message that I am trying to bring to the forefront of our thinking. Who cares what I think? God's Word matters. I hope you will grow in your desire to read the Bible by reading these devotionals.

Second, these devotionals are short. Thank God for the gifted teachers who have contributed to our understanding of the Bible by writing longer commentaries and works of theology. I read and benefit from many of these. I believe there is also a place for shorter writings that can shed light on God's Word to us. And I hope these devotionals will create an appetite in you for what those gifted teachers have given us in other books, and that you will read them, too.

Third, the devotionals refer often to the cross and the resurrection of Jesus Christ. Christianity is based on the message of God's grace. The grace of God refers to the salvation from sin that he provides for us through the death of his Son Jesus on the cross, and the resurrection of Jesus from the grave. As you read these devotionals, you will be reminded of the cross and resurrection of Jesus. And you will be called to respond to Jesus in repentance and faith.

Fourth, these devotionals make reference to the church. I am a pastor because I love the church of the Lord Jesus Christ. In these devotionals, I will regularly encourage you to read and discuss the Bible with others, to go to church, and to pray for your congregation. One of my main goals as a pastor is to help people come to a greater appreciation for and engagement with a local congregation. In congregations, the words of grace flow freely and give encouragement to all.

The *Words of Grace* devotionals are organized into three broad sections: Our Great God, God's Work in Our Lives, and Responding to God in Faith. These sections represent what I believe to be a helpful way of understanding what it means to be a Christian and to live as one. Everything about being a Christian begins with God, what he tells us about himself and his plan of salvation, and what he has done to provide for our salvation and life with him. We call this "grace" because it is a gift to us from God. When we see and hear what God shows us about himself and the salvation he provides, we are called to respond to him by faith. Faith is turning to God by trusting in his Son Jesus Christ and following Jesus as his disciple. The ordering of these devotionals is designed to help you live by grace through faith.

My prayer is that this devotional book will help you press the Word of God into your everyday life. As you read the Bible, may your mind be shaped by God's truth, your heart be stirred by his love, and your response to his grace be faith in the Lord Jesus.

## Section I

# Our Great God

## ——— Genesis 1:1 ———

In the beginning God created the heavens and the earth.

# God, the Author and Authority

The author has the authority. The writer of a book or a song stands over that work with complete freedom to edit and arrange it. The author can publish and perform the work or give permission for others to do so. He could decide to tuck the work away and keep it entirely for personal enjoyment. The creator is the owner and controller of the creation, and rightfully so.

"In the beginning God created the heavens and the earth." God never released his copyright on the creation. He is the author and has authority over all things.

God did not create only the physical world—the earth and all its material inhabitants. He is the author of the way things are supposed to be, including the way his creatures are to relate to him. God is the one who ordained that his own sovereign lordship over all things is to be acknowledged, honored, obeyed, and even enjoyed by those he created. The authority of God extends to the relationship he has with us.

So, what went wrong? Shortly after the creation, the first man and woman usurped the authority of God and acted as if they, and the serpent who tempted them, were the authors of the way things are to be. Their way seemed right to them rather than the way God had established. Their way introduced the chaos that is in the world, replacing the goodness of God's original design. Their way brought about the breach between the Creator and the created (Gen. 3).

The rebellion against the authority of God, and the breakdown that resulted, was so great that only God himself could restore creation to himself. So begins the biblical account of God's redeeming grace from Genesis 3 all the way to the end of the Revelation, the last book of the Bible.

This account of redeeming grace takes us through centuries, lands and nations, with prophets, kings and people, until we finally come to the Savior sent for sinners. This Savior restores the authority of God over his redeemed people, and will restore it over all creation by making all things new. The final scene in the Bible, showing us the final and eternal reality, is of the redeemed, joyfully living in the light of God's eternal rule over them (Rev. 21–22).

The biblical witness is that we have already shaken off God's gracious authority over us and have instead demanded our independence from him. The biblical question is, have we repented of this mutiny and turned to Jesus Christ, the Savior sent to bring us back under the rightful and benevolent authority of God our Creator?

Today, ask yourself, *Am I submitting to God as the Author and Authority of my life?*

## Genesis 1:26–31

Then God said, "Let us make man in our image, according to our likeness. They will rule the fish of the sea, the birds of the sky, the livestock, the whole earth, and the creatures that crawl on the earth."

So God created man
in his own image;
he created him in the image of God;
he created them male and female.

God blessed them, and God said to them, "Be fruitful, multiply, fill the earth, and subdue it. Rule the fish of the sea, the birds of the sky, and every creature that crawls on the earth." God also said, "Look, I have given you every seed-bearing plant on the surface of the entire earth and every tree whose fruit contains seed. This will be food for you, for all the wildlife of the earth, for every bird of the sky, and for every creature that crawls on the earth—everything having the breath of life in it—I have given every green plant for food." And it was so. God saw all that he had made, and it was very good indeed. Evening came and then morning: the sixth day.

# God and the Human Life He Created

The first thing the Bible reveals to us about God is his role as Creator. "In the beginning God created . . ." Our understanding of him must start here. Because he is Creator, he has authority—authority that we must respect. We must also respect that which he has created, for everything he creates is "good indeed."

Reverence for God as Creator and respect for the life he created form the foundation for every moral decision we face. We do not have one reason to abolish abortion and another to remove racism from our hearts; we do not have two different reasons for ending poverty and abhorring pornography. These, along with a multitude of other moral issues of our day, find their solution in one overriding truth: that God created all human life in his image and for his glory. When that truth grips our hearts, we will love so well that devaluing any life, at whatever stage and in whatever kind of skin, will no longer be an option.

Our nation is in constant conversation about race, abortion, poverty, violence, politics, and a host of other issues. How can Christians seek to offer a solution to any of these issues apart from reverence for God the Creator and respect for the human life he has created?

It seems that all moral roads lead back to Genesis 1:27: "So God created man in his own image."

Do you naturally revere God? Do you naturally respect the life he created *completely*? Does love of God and love of neighbor come easily for you? Certainly not. Sin resides in every human heart, rearing its ugly head in the form of disrespect for God and the devaluing of his image bearers. No one is morally perfect.

The gospel is the good news that God saves us in Christ from the sin that resides in our hearts, and that he works deeply in our souls to restore in us a reverence for himself and a respect for all human life.

The world around us is full of problems. It always will be, because it is full of sinful people. But Christians cannot be a worldly people who search for solutions in ourselves; we must rather be a kingdom people who search for answers in the Word of God and the gospel of Jesus Christ.

Do you have a healthy reverence of God as Creator of all? Do you love the human life he has created? If you are a Christian, the Holy Spirit is restoring this reverence and love in you. Open yourself up to the exposure of God's Word and Spirit. Cling to the gospel of God's grace in Christ that cleanses you from all sin.

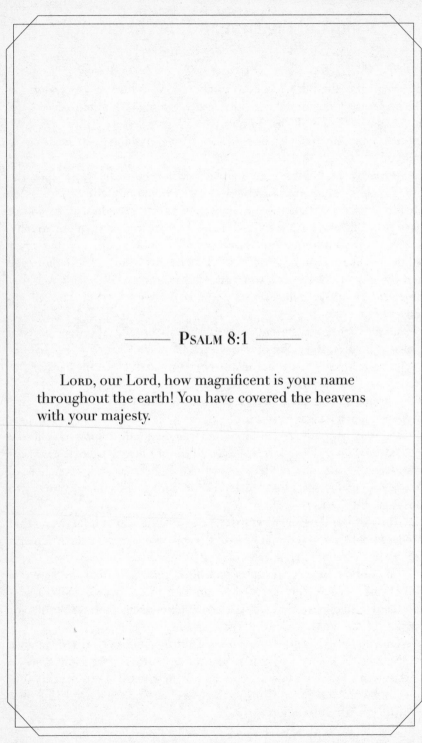

—— Psalm 8:1 ——

Lord, our Lord, how magnificent is your name throughout the earth! You have covered the heavens with your majesty.

# God and His Glory

David declared that God's name is magnificent throughout the earth, and that he has covered the heavens with his majesty (Ps. 8:1). Another rendering of this verse is that God has set his glory over and above all creation. The heavens and earth are not to be glorified. Their chief end is to glorify God. All praise of creation is actually a song about the perfection and power of the Creator.

It is interesting that we are created to experience and express glory, but that we seek our own glory in our creative works. Certainly, we should engage in creative activity. We were made in the image of God, who made things, so we make things too. But sometimes we make things to glorify ourselves instead of revealing the image of God in us.

Take the Tower of Babel, for example. Genesis 11 tells us that the inhabitants of the earth decided to build a city with a tower that reached high into the sky. We might think they were simply being creative, using imaginative powers, engineering skills, and city planning methods to make life on earth work. But the purpose of this tower was to make a name for the people. The tower was made for their glory. This is especially troublesome because the people had an awareness of God's glory in creation, but God's glory wasn't enough; they wanted their own.

Seeing only fireworks displayed against the backdrop of the night sky with shining moon and stars, or hearing only the music of a concert when thunder is booming around us can be metaphors for seeking our glory in light of God's. Seeking glory in our works in light of God's glory in creation is like cropping out the red rocks of Sedona or the redwoods of California from our selfie.

Our glory fades against the backdrop of God's creation. Have you ever seen a brightly lit building fade under the rising sun? God's glory is over and above the creation. So why don't we, or won't we, see God's glory? The flickering light of self-glory is so close to our eyes that it blinds us to the glory of the Lord. But this is a temporary phenomenon. For, "the glory of the LORD will appear, and all humanity together will see it" (Isa. 40:5).

Do you see the glory of the Lord? This will only happen through repentance and faith, seeing in the face of Jesus Christ the light of the knowledge of the glory of God (2 Cor. 4:6). Look to Jesus, the only Son of God sent to save us from our sin. He is the glory of God, and he will restore us to that good purpose for which we were created, to reflect glory back to him.

## ——— ROMANS 3:21–26 ———

But now, apart from the law, the righteousness of God has been revealed, attested by the Law and the Prophets. The righteousness of God is through faith in Jesus Christ to all who believe, since there is no distinction. For all have sinned and fall short of the glory of God. They are justified freely by his grace through the redemption that is in Christ Jesus. God presented him as an atoning sacrifice in his blood, received through faith, to demonstrate his righteousness, because in his restraint God passed over the sins previously committed. God presented him to demonstrate his righteousness at the present time, so that he would be righteous and declare righteous the one who has faith in Jesus.

# God, the Just and Justifier

Romans 3:21–26 is considered by many to be the most important paragraph on salvation in the Bible. All the realities of human need and God's grace are present in these words. God's righteousness is said to be revealed to us. God's righteousness has for centuries been understood by readers of Romans as his right way of making sinners right with himself.

In this passage is the straightforward affirmation that all humans are sinners, fallen in their nature, coming up short of God's glory. We don't know or honor God's glory, nor do we reflect it as we were created to do. We dishonor God and seek self-glory (Rom. 1).

Then we see the way God dealt with our sin. He sent his Son, Jesus Christ, to be the atoning sacrifice for our sins. As such, when Jesus died on the cross he took our sins to himself, bore the punishment of God against our sin in his body, and thereby freed us from condemnation for our sin. God sent Jesus to be our substitute. This is the definition of grace.

The application of Christ's substitutionary death to the individual person is also explained. It is by faith that what Jesus did on the cross is applied to a person. The righteousness of God—God making a person right with himself—is through faith in Jesus Christ to all who believe.

The paragraph closes with the declaration that God, by means of this plan of salvation, is righteous and declares righteous the one who has faith in Jesus. Another way to say this is that God is just and the justifier of those who trust in Jesus.

Something important to notice about the plan of salvation laid out in this passage is what it says about the nature of God. God is just. There is nothing about his plan of salvation that is unfair, unjust, or open to criticism. If God's plan is not received well by us, it is not the fault of the plan, but another bit of evidence that we are not just, as he is.

God is the justifier. To be the justifier, God must be the judge. "The LORD sits enthroned forever, he has established his throne for judgment. And he judges the world with righteousness; he executes judgment on the nations with fairness" (Ps. 9:7–8).

Before God's plan of salvation in the substitutionary death of Jesus was revealed, we were left wondering how anyone could stand before God who judges in righteousness. Now that the plan has been revealed, we are led to repentance of sin, faith in Christ, humility before the cross, peace before the throne of God, and freedom to live for his glory now.

God is just. Is he your justifier? Have you repented of your sin before him? Do you believe and receive his Son today?

## PSALM 62:11–12

God has spoken once; I have heard this twice: strength belongs to God, and faithful love belongs to you, LORD. For you repay each according to his works.

# God Is Great and Good

Strength belongs to the Lord. Power is his. King David was certain of this truth, for twice he heard it from the Lord.

The subject of God's power has been much discussed. Can God make a rock so big that even he can't move it? Maybe that's a silly question, but it raises a serious issue. Does God's power ever create a conflict within him? The short answer is, *No*. God is perfect, so he is never in a dilemma that leaves him trying to figuring out his next move.

A question a bit closer to home is, *Can we trust a God who possesses all power?* This raises the question, *Is God raw power?* Are there any other influences within the character of God that govern even the use of his power? Is there anything to comfort us in the knowledge of God's power?

David not only heard twice that strength belongs to the Lord, but also that faithful love is his. When God exercises his strength in the Bible, he is also expressing his love and goodness. The power to create was used to bring about a good world. After each day's work, God saw that it was good. The arm of the Lord against the Egyptians delivered the Israelites for his good purpose and their good future. The resurrection of Jesus from the grave by the exercise of God's power is the victory over death and the good gift of life to us.

God's greatness and goodness are inseparable. Whatever he chooses to do with his power can be trusted to be for good. As the psalm says, he is good and he does good (Ps. 119:68).

Nowhere is the greatness and goodness of God more evident than at the cross of Jesus Christ. The cross is great because it is the place where the power of Christ's perfect life became the sacrifice for our sins to satisfy its penalty on our behalf. As the hymn says, "There is power in the blood of the Lamb."[1]

The cross is good because the accomplishment of it is granted to us by grace through faith. The exercise of God's power was on our behalf. The satisfaction of the sentence of death for sin was counted as ours. Union with Christ is real. His death is ours—his life too. This is pure goodness and a gracious gift.

"God is great and God is good, let us thank him for our food," goes the children's prayer before the meal. The prayer of thanksgiving to our great and good God for the cross of Christ is prayed each day by the Christian, and each Lord's Day by the church gathered to worship him who has redeemed and restored us to himself.

Yes, the great God can be trusted because he is also good. He is shown to be so in his Son. Do you know this great and good God? Do you know his great and good salvation? Are you making his greatness and goodness known to others with a congregation of God's people? Think on these things.

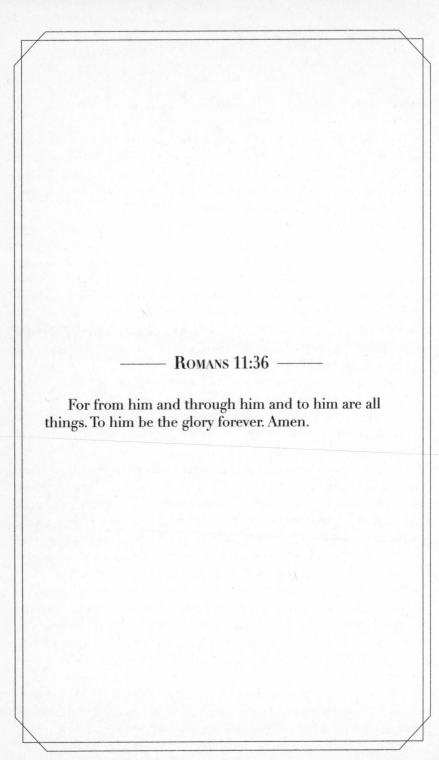

## ROMANS 11:36

For from him and through him and to him are all things. To him be the glory forever. Amen.

# God Over All Things

Under the inspiration of the Holy Spirit, and after a long meditation on the righteous of God in the plan of salvation, the apostle Paul declared, "For from him and through him and to him are all things. To him be the glory forever. Amen." Could there be a more succinct yet all-encompassing statement about the place of God in relation to all things that exist?

From him—God is the creator of all things. "In the beginning God created the heavens and the earth" (Gen. 1:1). From God, through his Son, flows grace upon grace by which he redeems sinners and will restore all things for his purposes (John 1:16).

Through him—God keeps all things in existence through his power and for his purposes. "In him all things hold together" (Col. 1:17 ESV).

To him—All things were created for God's glory and to him will be the glory forever. Amen.

If there is one great truth at the foundation of all truth, it is that God is over all things. And the truth that shapes how we live as Christians is that God is over and connected to all aspects of our lives.

In the realm of morality and money, family and friends, work and play, God has a will and a way for us to live. Working this truth out in real life is challenging and requires prayer and wisdom. The way is not always easy to discern, but we must exercise our spiritual mind muscle to do so. Creative and decisive obedience to God's purposes in every area of life is called for. Jesus prayed this for us. "Sanctify them in truth; your word is truth" (John 17:17 ESV).

Christians are not to divide our lives into spiritual and unspiritual categories, as if God applies to some parts and not to others. When we do this, we end up "putting God in his place" and setting ourselves up as lord of every other place. God then is relegated to church, ceremonies, and holidays, while in everything else we are on our own.

This is no way to live, nor will it lead to life. One reason Christians do not know much of the joy Jesus prayed we would know (John 17:13) is because we live as if God is over some things, not all things. We are still holding out on God and holding on to some things for ourselves. We are keeping God at a safe distance, so we think, by keeping him in the safe places of our lives.

The Bible shows us the God who is Lord over all, for all things are from, through, and to him. The way to joy in God is to know God as he is. Rivers of joy flood the soul and flow out in love to God when he is declared over all things in life and in our lives. Recognize today that God is over all things, and live in light of this great truth.

## 1 Corinthians 13:1–13

If I speak human or angelic tongues but do not have love, I am a noisy gong or a clanging cymbal. If I have the gift of prophecy and understand all mysteries and all knowledge, and if I have all faith so that I can move mountains but do not have love, I am nothing. And if I give away all my possessions, and if I give over my body in order to boast but do not have love, I gain nothing.

Love is patient, love is kind. Love does not envy, is not boastful, is not arrogant, is not rude, is not self-seeking, is not irritable, and does not keep a record of wrongs. Love finds no joy in unrighteousness but rejoices in the truth. It bears all things, believes all things, hopes all things, endures all things.

Love never ends. But as for prophecies, they will come to an end; as for tongues, they will cease; as for knowledge, it will come to an end. For we know in part, and we prophesy in part, but when the perfect comes, the partial will come to an end. When I was a child, I spoke like a child, I thought like a child, I reasoned like a child. When I became a man, I put aside childish things. For now we see only a reflection as in a mirror, but then face to face. Now I know in part, but then I will know fully, as I am fully known. Now these three remain: faith, hope, and love—but the greatest of these is love.

# The Love of God

English-speaking people have one word for many kinds of affection. The word *love* is used for food, sports, and spouses. It applies to marital fidelity and fornication. The only way to know what it means when it is used is to listen for the context or watch for the facial expression of the one speaking. In English, *love* covers a multitude of feelings.

The Greeks had different words to refer to different loves. Friendship love and sexual love had their own words. The New Testament (written in Greek) uses a special word that almost exclusively refers to God's love. That word is *agape.*

Agape is used to refer to the love that God has for us. This love was demonstrated when God sent Jesus Christ to die for our sins so that we would be forgiven and reconciled to him. God's love is in a category of its own. It gets its own word.

Agape refers to the nature of the God who loves, not to the loveliness of the ones who are loved. If I say I love a song, I am telling you as much about the song as I am about myself. But to speak of God's agape love is to say something only about God. Agape refers to the God who loves us in Christ.

First Corinthians 13 is all about agape. It's about God's love, so it's about God. The common assumption is that we are to show agape to others. But how can that be? How can we, sinful and flawed humans, express the kind of love that points to the goodness of God? How can we say or do anything that refers to our ability to love like God?

This mystery is great, and it is resolved in the love of God itself. God, who loved us in Christ by sending him to die for our sins on the cross, also loves us by saving us from our sins and giving us new life. He raised Jesus from the dead and gives new life to all who repent and believe. This new life includes the ongoing transformation of our minds and hearts—of our deepest affections. The transformation is not immediate; in fact, it is painfully slow. But it is real. It is happening in all who are born of God's Spirit.

As God in Christ by the Spirit transforms us more and more, we love with his love (agape) more and more. We are changed by his love, and we begin to express his love to others. As new people in Christ, when we love with the love of God, we are not putting the spotlight on our love but on the one who first loved us.

Drink deeply today from the love of God, and pray that the Holy Spirit would continue to empower you to love others with the love God has shown you.

Therefore, since we have been declared righteous by faith, we have peace with God through our Lord Jesus Christ. We have also obtained access through him by faith into this grace in which we stand, and we rejoice in the hope of the glory of God. And not only that, but we also rejoice in our afflictions, because we know that affliction produces endurance, endurance produces proven character, and proven character produces hope. This hope will not disappoint us, because God's love has been poured out in our hearts through the Holy Spirit who was given to us.

For while we were still helpless, at the right time, Christ died for the ungodly. For rarely will someone die for a just person—though for a good person perhaps someone might even dare to die. But God proves his own love for us in that while we were still sinners, Christ died for us. How much more then, since we have now been declared righteous by his blood, will we be saved through him from wrath. For if, while we were enemies, we were reconciled to God through the death of his Son, then how much more, having been reconciled, will we be saved by his life. And not only that, but we also rejoice in God through our Lord Jesus Christ, through whom we have now received this reconciliation.

# Know the Love of God

"To know the love of God is indeed heaven on earth. The New Testament sets forth this knowledge, not as the privilege of a favored few, but as a normal part of ordinary Christian experience, something to which only the spiritually unhealthy and malformed will be strangers."[2]

God wants us to know his love. The apostle Paul wrote a prayer to that end. He prayed for the Ephesian Christians (a prayer we are encouraged to take as for ourselves as well) that they would know how long, wide, high, and deep is God's love. He prayed that they would know Christ's love that is beyond anyone's full comprehension (Eph. 3:14–19).

Why do we need to know the love of God? That phrase, "to know God's love," is a kind of code language for coming to know God himself, through faith in Jesus Christ. To know the love of God is to be saved from our sins and reconciled to him. It is to be filled with assurance before God and full of the life of God. To know God's love is to love God and live obediently for his glory. God's love in us is a flowing river of love for others.

How do we know the love of God? Romans 5:1–11 gives us two ways God himself has loved us and communicated his love for us. First, he sent his Son to be the sacrifice for our sins. While we were yet sinners, Christ died for us. To know the love of God, we must see it in the cross of Christ. A sinner kneels before the cross in humility, repentance, and faith, and finds the deep love of God. A Christian remains kneeling before the cross of Christ in continued amazement of this great demonstration of love. Faith in Christ is how we come to know this love.

Along with the great display of God's love in the cross of Christ, we have the internal witness of God's love through his Spirit, who was given to us. When we are born again, the Spirit of God comes to live in us, making us alive to God. The Spirit constantly communicates to us that God loves us and will always love us in Christ. The Spirit reminds us that nothing will separate us from the love of God.

We also have the written Word of God, the Bible. It is in the Bible that we read of the cross of Christ and the gift of the Spirit. The Holy Spirit is helping us see with new eyes the meaning of the cross and the depths of God's love that are in the Bible. The cross, the Spirit, and the Bible lead us into a deep knowledge of God's love.

Today, receive the love of God at the cross and through the Spirit. Repent and believe. Take up your Bible, open and read. Read it with someone who has not come to faith in Jesus. Read it with a fellow church member who needs encouragement. Know the love of God as the "normal part of ordinary Christian experience."

The next day, John was standing with two of his disciples. When he saw Jesus passing by, he said, "Look, the Lamb of God!"

The two disciples heard him say this and followed Jesus. When Jesus turned and noticed them following him, he asked them, "What are you looking for?"

They said to him, "Rabbi" (which means "Teacher"), "where are you staying?"

"Come and you'll see," he replied. So they went and saw where he was staying, and they stayed with him that day. It was about four in the afternoon.

Andrew, Simon Peter's brother, was one of the two who heard John and followed him. He first found his own brother Simon and told him, "We have found the Messiah" (which is translated "the Christ"), and he brought Simon to Jesus.

When Jesus saw him, he said, "You are Simon, Son of John. You will be called Cephas" (which is translated "Peter").

The next day Jesus decided to leave for Galilee. He found Philip and told him, "Follow me."

Now Philip was from Bethsaida, the hometown of Andrew and Peter. Philip found Nathanael and told him, "We have found the one Moses wrote about in the law (and so did the prophets): Jesus the son of Joseph, from Nazareth."

"Can anything good come out of Nazareth?" Nathanael asked him.

"Come and see," Philip answered.

# Meeting Jesus

Jesus came to be met.

So many people don't realize this. To them, Jesus is a figure in history, long dead and irrelevant, or the inspiration for discontent cultural revolutionaries, or the leader of morally uptight Americans. But a person to be met and known?

In the opening chapter of John's Gospel, we learn of the coming of Jesus. Grand statements about him are made in this chapter. The Word was in the beginning. The Word was with God from eternity. The Word was God. Jesus is this Word, which became a man and lived among us. Jesus is God and man in one person.

John 1 goes on to tell us that Jesus met people, and people actually met him. It tells us that we, too, can meet him.

How can we meet a man who lived two thousand years ago? Jesus is alive and he relates to us by his Spirit. He has given us information about himself in the Bible. He still speaks to us through the Bible. He gave us minds that can think, desires that lead to decisions, and bodies that can be used for service. Put all of this together, and we see how we can meet Jesus.

Meeting Jesus starts when he, by his Spirit, speaks to us from his Word. We then understand the words about Jesus, believe in him, decide to follow him, and make it our mission to serve him. Meeting Jesus happens because Jesus introduces himself to us, and we respond to him in faith.

Our lives should be saturated with this one, overarching goal: to meet Jesus. He has already introduced himself to you in his Word. I hope you will continue to meet him there.

When the eight days were completed for his circumcision, he was named Jesus—the name given by the angel before he was conceived. And when the days of their purification according to the law of Moses were finished, they brought him up to Jerusalem to present him to the Lord (just as it is written in the law of the Lord, Every firstborn male will be dedicated to the Lord) and to offer a sacrifice (according to what is stated in the law of the Lord, a pair of turtledoves or two young pigeons).

There was a man in Jerusalem whose name was Simeon. This man was righteous and devout, looking forward to Israel's consolation, and the Holy Spirit was on him. It had been revealed to him by the Holy Spirit that he would not see death before he saw the Lord's Messiah. Guided by the Spirit, he entered the temple. When the parents brought in the child Jesus to perform for him what was customary under the law, Simeon took him up in his arms, praised God, and said,

Now, Master,
you can dismiss your servant in peace,
as you promised.
For my eyes have seen
your salvation.
You have prepared it
in the presence of all peoples—
a light for revelation to the Gentiles
and glory to your people Israel.

# The Beauty of Our Savior in the Song of Simeon

Simeon was a unique man. He had the experience of being told by the Holy Spirit that before he died he would see the Messiah. One day in the temple, Simeon saw Jesus being carried by his parents. He took one look into the face of Jesus and recognized him. Here, in the baby, was the Messiah. Simeon broke out in song and sang a prophecy of the beauty of Christ.

In the face of Jesus, Simeon saw the salvation of the world. Human history is the search for saviors. Everyone has the sense that things aren't quite right and that we need someone to fix the world. The driving force behind politics, religion, art, and entertainment is the desire for someone to stand up, point the way, and lead us to a better future.

Jesus Christ stepped into human history. The Son of God became a human. In Jesus' infancy, Simeon was able to see in him the Savior we need to make the world right. He was called "a light for revelation to the Gentiles." This means he revealed God and God's way of salvation to all the nations.

It is clear from the teaching of the Bible that the Savior of the world is the Savior of the individual who repents of sin and turns to Jesus in faith for salvation. In the face of Jesus, Simeon saw his own salvation. You can too. Turn to Jesus now and trust him to save you.

What does it take to see Jesus the way Simeon did? How can we come to the place of seeing in Jesus the greatest satisfaction of our souls?

First, pray that God will let you see Jesus this way. It is God who opened Simeon's mind to understand that Jesus was no ordinary baby. Ask God to do this in you as well.

Second, think about your own life. Doesn't everything you have ever seen or experienced fall short of perfect? Doesn't every relationship come with a little disappointment? The reason this is so is that we were made for Christ, and nothing satisfies us like knowing and loving him, and knowing we are loved by him.

Third, think on Jesus. Finding your soul's joy in Jesus Christ requires deep soul reflection. We won't have joy if we constantly medicate dissatisfaction with superficial things. We must think deeply on Jesus—his superior nature and sufficient work on the cross.

Simeon sang of the beauty of Jesus and declared him to be the Savior who fully satisfies all who believe. Believe in him and be satisfied by the beauty of our Savior.

## LUKE 3:15–22

Now the people were waiting expectantly, and all of them were questioning in their hearts whether John might be the Messiah. John answered them all, "I baptize you with water, but the one who is more powerful than I am is coming. I am not worthy to untie the strap of his sandals. He will baptize you with the Holy Spirit and fire. His winnowing shovel is in his hand to clear his threshing floor and gather the wheat into his barn, but the chaff he will burn with fire that never goes out." Then, along with many other exhortations, he proclaimed good news to the people. But when John rebuked Herod the tetrarch because of Herodias, his brother's wife, and all the evil things he had done, Herod added this to everything else—he locked up John in prison.

When all the people were baptized, Jesus also was baptized. As he was praying, heaven opened, and the Holy Spirit descended on him in a physical appearance like a dove. And a voice came from heaven: "You are my beloved Son; with you I am well-pleased."

# The Beauty of Our Savior in His Baptism

When John the Baptist looked into the face of Jesus, he saw the One "who is more powerful than I" (Luke 3:16). John knew Jesus to be the One Isaiah spoke of when he said, "all humanity together will see" the glory of the Lord (Isa. 40:5). So John must have been startled when Jesus came to him to be baptized. What is the mighty One doing being baptized? Baptism is for sinners, not Saviors.

Therein lies the beauty of our Savior. He became one of us. Jesus stepped into the waters of baptism as an act of prophecy; he was declaring his death, burial, and resurrection. His baptism was an act of submission—he was doing what the Father commanded him to do, even though he did not need the baptism of repentance for himself. And, by being baptized, Jesus was identifying with the sinful humanity he came to save.

In his baptism, Jesus was pointing to the cross of his death where he would become sin on our behalf. There he would take the wrath of God for our sin in his own body, and thereby win freedom and righteousness for us.

John the Baptist not only baptized Jesus but he also prophesied that Jesus would baptize us in the Holy Spirit and fire. John said Jesus was "coming" to do this. This is why he came to earth. His baptizing us in the Holy Spirit is the reason for his coming to us as a baby. When Simeon saw the baby (Luke 2:28) and John saw the man to be baptized, they both saw the same thing—a beautiful Savior.

The first few chapters of Luke's Gospel tell us all about the reason for Christ's coming. Luke is telling us that the purpose of the Son of God taking on the form of a baby at this birth and of Jesus stepping into the waters of baptism are the same. He was identifying with us by becoming one of us in order to offer himself for us on the cross, so that he may baptize us in the Holy Spirit.

So what does that mean? Luke also wrote the book of Acts. There, we see the work of the Holy Spirit in the lives of the first followers of Jesus. The Holy Spirit filled them with new life and power. He animated them, motivated them, gave them power, was the constant presence of God among them, helped them in their weakness to be pure, made them bold for witness, gave them gifts for ministry, and guided their steps in life and mission. Just as Jesus was God among them, so the Holy Spirit is God in them (Rom. 8:9–11).

The biblical witness is that a person is baptized in the Holy Spirit at the moment of conversion, which is by faith in Christ. To be saved by Jesus is to have the Spirit of Jesus. Jesus is a beautiful Savior, and the baptism of the Holy Spirit is his gift to us. Repent of your sins, believe on his name, and receive him by faith.

He came to Nazareth, where he had been brought up. As usual, he entered the synagogue on the Sabbath day and stood up to read. The scroll of the prophet Isaiah was given to him, and unrolling the scroll, he found the place where it was written:
The Spirit of the Lord is on me,
because he has anointed me
to preach good news to the poor.
He has sent me
to proclaim release
to the captives
and recovery of sight to the blind,
to set free the oppressed,
to proclaim the year
of the Lord's favor.
He then rolled up the scroll, gave it back to the attendant, and sat down. And the eyes of everyone in the synagogue were fixed on him. He began by saying to them, "Today as you listen, this Scripture has been fulfilled."

# The Beauty of Our Savior in His Own Words

For the past few days, we have seen the beauty of Jesus in the prophecies of the early chapters of Luke. There was Simeon in the temple. He saw the baby Jesus, took him in his arms, and sang a song of salvation. In Jesus, Simeon saw and proclaimed the light of revelation to the Gentiles and the glory of Israel (Luke 2:32).

Then there was John at the Jordan. He saw the man Jesus, took him in his arms, and baptized him. In Jesus, John saw and proclaimed the One who was mightier than he, and who would baptize us in the Holy Spirit and fire (Luke 3:16).

The next prophecy Luke records concerning Jesus is the one made by Jesus himself. Like Simeon and John, Jesus looked to Isaiah for his prophecy. Jesus went into the synagogue, took the book of the prophet Isaiah in his arms, and read to the congregation. In Isaiah, Jesus saw himself and proclaimed his reason for coming (Luke 4:18–19).

The beauty of Jesus is seen fully in the final words of the prophecy: Jesus had come to proclaim "the year of the Lord's favor." This phrase is a reference to the Year of Jubilee mentioned in Leviticus 25. The Lord gave instructions that every fiftieth year was to be the year of release. If a person was in debt and had sold himself to another to pay off the debt, he was released from servitude and debt at the year of Jubilee. Each person was to return to his own property and to his own family. The favor of the Lord had released him.

Jesus used Isaiah to refer to himself as the Preacher of good news. What was the message of good news? God's favor is on all mankind. The year of release is here. Jesus himself is the Releaser. He has come to the poor, the captives, the sick, and the oppressed to announce that in him God is smiling on them. God is here in Jesus to set people free from all that binds them and keeps them from knowing his grace, glory, and love.

For Jesus, the prophecy of God's favor toward people came with a price for him to pay. Release for captives and forgiveness for sinners is not free. As Jesus proclaimed the Jubilee year for us, he knew there was a bitter cup of crucifixion for himself. There he paid our debts. There he bore our sins. There on the cross he took the wrath of God for our transgressions and declared, "it is finished."

Now, all who call upon the name of the Lord are saved. All who turn to him for salvation are released from sin's condemnation and oppression. All who trust him enter the Year of Jubilee where the favorable smile of God is forever enjoyed.

Alleluia, what a beautiful Savior!

## —— JOHN 13:1–5, 12–17 ——

Before the Passover Festival, Jesus knew that his hour had come to depart from this world to the Father. Having loved his own who were in the world, he loved them to the end.

Now when it was time for supper, the devil had already put it into the heart of Judas, Simon Iscariot's son, to betray him. Jesus knew that the Father had given everything into his hands, that he had come from God, and that he was going back to God. So he got up from supper, laid aside his outer clothing, took a towel, and tied it around himself. Next, he poured water into a basin and began to wash his disciples' feet and to dry them with the towel tied around him.

When Jesus had washed their feet and put on his outer clothing, he reclined again and said to them, "Do you know what I have done for you? You call me Teacher and Lord—and you are speaking rightly, since that is what I am. So if I, your Lord and Teacher, have washed your feet, you also ought to wash one another's feet. For I have given you an example, that you also should do just as I have done for you.

"Truly I tell you, a servant is not greater than his master, and a messenger is not greater than the one who sent him. If you know these things, you are blessed if you do them."

# Awed by Humility

Mountains, oceans, and views into space inspire a deep sense of wonder in us. Grand human achievements in art and science and great acts of heroism grab our attention. In theology, the "omnis" of God's nature (all knowing, all present, all powerful) elevate our thoughts of him to the highest levels. We were made with the capacity for awe, and we are given plenty of reasons to experience and express it.

But sometimes, the most awesome things we behold are not the most grandiose. In fact, we can be most awed by humility, especially when it is seen in Jesus. The account of Jesus stooping to wash the disciples' feet in John 13 is an awesome display of humility.

Envision the scene in your mind. Jesus lays aside his outer garment, takes up a towel, and wraps it around his waist. The King of Creation pours water in a basin, kneels down in front of twelve men, and washes their feet one by one. Jesus becomes the servant.

A sense of gratitude should come over us knowing that this act of humility foreshadowed the cross that would come in just a few hours. There, Jesus would perform the greatest act of service. He would die to cleanse us of our sin.

When God came near, he did so in Jesus Christ, who stooped to serve twelve men by washing their feet, and you and me by dying on a cross.

Today, remember that the truly awe-inspiring event of history is the coming of Christ. He humbled himself through a human birth, a manger scene, a life of obedience, a bloody cross, and the cleansing of a people he would call his own.

## Philippians 2:5–6

Adopt the same attitude as that of Christ Jesus, who, existing in the form of God, did not consider equality with God as something to be exploited.

## John 13:1–3

Before the Passover Festival, Jesus knew that his hour had come to depart from this world to the Father. Having loved his own who were in the world, he loved them to the end. Now when it was time for supper, the devil had already put it into the heart of Judas, Simon Iscariot's son, to betray him. Jesus knew that the Father had given everything into his hands, that he had come from God, and that he was going back to God.

# His Thinking

What was Jesus thinking? We see in the Gospels what he did and we hear what he taught, but what was in his mind? The answer is that he was considering his identity and his purpose, and how he would accomplish it.

Jesus Christ is eternally God the Son, enjoying perfect union and fellowship with God the Father and God the Spirit. He knew that the plan of God was to save a people for himself from out of the world. He knew that he, as the Son, was to take on humanity in order to deal with the sin problem of humans. He knew he would suffer the death sentence for sin on their behalf. Thinking about all of this, he "did not consider equality with God as something to be exploited." He thought about his state of being as God the Son with privileges, rights, and power and without humanity, limitation, and temptation, and regarded this as something that needed to be laid aside in order to bring about salvation. Jesus thought of himself as a servant.

John 13 gives us a picture of the Son of God who took on humanity, serving his disciples by washing their feet. But here, too, we are told what Jesus was thinking before the foot washing.

He knew that the time had come for him to leave this world. He knew that God the Father had put the decision to go to the cross in his hands. He knew that he had come from the Father for the purpose of the cross. He knew that before the cross, one of his disciples would betray him and the others would desert him. And he knew that, after his death on the cross, he would be raised from the dead. Knowing all of this, he washed their feet.

The foot washing was more than a practical act; it was a prophetic act. Yes, the service he rendered was cleaning feet, but that only pointed to the greater service of giving people a clean heart through the cross that awaited him.

These windows into the thinking of Jesus show us how we, the followers of Christ, are to think of ourselves and act toward each other. We are to have the mind of Christ among ourselves. Think on these things.

## PHILIPPIANS 2:7–8

Instead he emptied himself by assuming the form of a servant, taking on the likeness of humanity. And when he had come as a man, he humbled himself by becoming obedient to the point of death—even to death on a cross.

## JOHN 13:4

So he got up from supper, laid aside his outer clothing, took a towel, and tied it around himself.

# His Laying Aside

We know someone's commitment to a purpose or a cause by what he or she is willing to give up for it.

Philippians 2 shows us that the Son of God was totally committed to the purpose of saving sinners because he made himself nothing. He emptied himself. This means that Jesus gave up something. He laid something aside.

John 13 gives us the account of Jesus washing the disciples' feet the night before he died. I've often wondered about the detailed description of this event. Each action of Jesus is supplied. He rose from supper, he laid aside his outer garments, he took up a towel and wrapped it around his waist, he poured water into a basin, he washed their feet, and he wiped them with the towel.

John must have a reason for telling us each step Jesus took at this foot washing. I believe we are supposed to consider each step in light of the actions Christ took to secure our salvation.

See it in your mind's eye. Jesus rose from supper and laid aside his outer garment. At that moment, he was committing himself to wash their feet. Why else would he have shed his garment? He's "all in" at this point.

The Son of God, in committing himself to accomplish our salvation on the cross, "emptied himself." He let go of and laid aside his heavenly glory and the privileges he enjoyed as God the Son. He was committed to the purpose of bringing glory to God by showing grace to sinners.

After washing the disciples' feet, Jesus put back on his outer garment and resumed his place at the table. After the cross, he took back up his glory and ascended back into heaven. But only after he accomplished the purpose of saving a people out of the world for God.

Today, as you consider Jesus, can you think of other times recorded in the Gospels when he laid aside the glory that was his in heaven in order to accomplish his purpose on earth?

## PHILIPPIANS 2:7–8

Instead he emptied himself by assuming the form of a servant, taking on the likeness of humanity. And when he had come as a man, he humbled himself by becoming obedient to the point of death—even to death on a cross.

## JOHN 13:5

Next, he poured water into a basin and began to wash his disciples' feet and to dry them with the towel tied around him.

# His Taking On

It is hard to speak of Jesus Christ, the Son of God, as a servant. Personally, I am only comfortable doing so because the Old Testament prophet Isaiah spoke of the Servant of the Lord as the Messiah, Jesus referred to himself as one who came to serve (Mark 10:45), and the service he rendered is unique.

Jesus Christ took on the form of a servant. Don't let the language trip you up. "Assuming the form of a servant" doesn't mean that he appeared to be a servant but really wasn't or that he dressed up like a servant but was pretending. It means he remained fully God and at the same time became a man and a servant.

In John 13 we see Jesus serving in an embarrassingly crude way. Granted, people in Jesus' day had their feet washed by household servants, but the owner of the house did not do the washing. A Jew would never have been expected to do such a task. So for Jesus, both the master and a Jew, to wash the disciples' feet was crude. It embarrassed the disciples because they should have provided for this task to be done for Jesus, rather than him doing it for them.

Jesus doesn't see himself as above the task, nor is he embarrassed to perform it. The only explanation for this is that he became a servant. He took on the identity and the role of a servant. He was doing what servants do.

What Jesus did in the foot washing was practical in that he cleaned feet and showed us that we too can serve others. But it was also prophetic in that he was pointing to the ultimate act of service he would carry out on the cross. There on the cross, the Servant carried our sorrows and bore the sin of many (Isa. 53).

Have you received the service of Jesus offered to you, or are you resisting the embarrassment of needing to have your feet washed?

Are you following the pattern of discipleship given to us by Jesus? Are you a servant?

## Philippians 2:7b–8

And when he had come as a man, he humbled himself by becoming obedient to the point of death — even to death on a cross.

## John 13:6–8

He came to Simon Peter, who asked him, "Lord, are you going to wash my feet?"

Jesus answered him, "What I'm doing you don't realize now, but afterward you will understand."

"You will never wash my feet," Peter said.

# His Obedience

Jesus prayed to God the Father and said that he had accomplished the work given him to do (John 17:4). What was that work? "Carrying the cross by himself, he went out to what is called Place of the Skull, which in Aramaic is called *Golgotha*. There they crucified him" (John 19:17–18). This was his work.

When Jesus was washing the disciples' feet, they did not understand that he was giving them a sign of the soul cleansing he would provide through his death. He knew it, though. He told them they would come to understand the cleansing nature of death in due time (John 13:6–8).

The Son of God knew the cross was his destination from the time he decided to lay aside the glory of heaven, become a man, and assume the role of a servant. Everything he thought and did was unto the cross. And since the cross was the work the Father gave him to do, everything he thought and did was in obedience. In the cross we see the obedience unto death that is unique to Jesus. He alone was fully obedient. He alone could die for the forgiveness of sins.

Think today on the obedience of Jesus in his death on the cross. The sense we get from being confronted by the cross of Christ is one of a pricked conscience. His cross was in our place and for our sin. Away with a lighthearted attitude about our rebellion against a holy God! Christ's death was the only death sufficient to pay for such an offense, because he is the only one who perfectly obeyed God and didn't need someone to pay for his sin.

The sense we get from embracing the cross of Christ is one of a peaceful conscience. Our sins are covered, removed, and cast away because Jesus bore the wrath of God against them. Through repentance and faith, our sins are no longer counted against us. Away with the dark cloud of condemnation that threatens to undo us!

> My sin—oh, the bliss of this glorious thought!
> My sin, not in part but the whole
> Is nailed to the cross, and I bear it no more;
> Praise the Lord, praise the Lord, O my soul![3]

## PHILIPPIANS 2:9

For this reason God highly exalted him and gave him the name that is above every name.

## JOHN 20:11–17

But Mary stood outside the tomb, crying. As she was crying, she stooped to look into the tomb. She saw two angels in white sitting where Jesus's body had been lying, one at the head and the other at the feet. They said to her, "Woman, why are you crying?"

"Because they've taken away my Lord," she told them, "and I don't know where they've put him."

Having said this, she turned around and saw Jesus standing there, but she did not know it was Jesus. "Woman," Jesus said to her, "why are you crying? Who is it that you're seeking."

Supposing he was the gardener, she replied, "Sir, if you've carried him away, tell me where you've put him, and I will take him away."

Jesus said to her, "Mary."

Turning around, she said to him in Aramaic, "Rabboni!"—which means "Teacher."

"Don't cling to me," Jesus told her, "since I have not yet ascended to the Father. But go to my brothers and tell them that I am ascending to my Father and your Father, to my God and your God."

# His Exaltation

It was hard enough for those who followed Jesus to mentally and emotionally deal with his crucifixion. They certainly were not expecting his resurrection. But Jesus told them that both would happen. And he spoke of his crucifixion and resurrection as if they were part of one single event (Mark 8:31).

Philippians 2 tells us the connection. Because Jesus humbled himself by becoming obedient to the point of death on a cross, God highly exalted him. The exaltation of Jesus began with his resurrection from the dead.

John gives us one of the resurrection accounts recorded in the Gospels (John 20:11–17). In this account Mary Magdalene, a follower of Jesus, comes to the tomb and sees that the stone has been rolled away from the entrance and that Jesus' body is gone. She does not immediately think of a resurrection. She thinks someone has taken his body to another location.

But Jesus calls her name, and she recognizes him. With joy she takes hold of Jesus, but he tells her not to cling to him, because he has not yet ascended to the Father.

What do we make of this resurrection and the talk of ascension? The plan of God, which we have already seen included the death of Jesus, also included the exaltation of Jesus, through his resurrection and ascension into heaven (Luke 24:50–52). Jesus is highly exalted as Lord.

After Mary saw Jesus alive and heard him say he would ascend to the Father, she went and announced to the disciples, "I have seen the Lord."

We don't have to look any further than in the pages of the Gospels to see the exalted Lord of the universe. Jesus is Lord.

## PHILIPPIANS 2:9–11

For this reason God highly exalted him and gave him the name that is above every name, so that at the name of Jesus every knee will bow—in heaven and on earth and under the earth—and every tongue will confess that Jesus Christ is Lord, to the glory of God the Father.

## JOHN 20:18

Mary Magdalene went and announced to the disciples, "I have seen the Lord!" And she told them what he had said to her.

# His Lordship

Jesus is Lord. Mary Magdalene was given the ability to see that Jesus is Lord, and she was the first to confess his lordship after he was raised from the dead (John 20:18).

What does it mean for Jesus to be Lord? God the Father bestowed on Jesus Christ the designation of Lord. This makes Jesus' lordship unique; he alone is Lord.

Jesus' lordship is tied up in his humble obedience to the point of death on the cross and in his resurrection from the dead to the point of ascension into heaven. Since these acts are for our salvation, Jesus' lordship means he is our Savior. Jesus saved us to be a people for his own possession who are zealous for good works (Titus 2:14). Jesus as our Lord means we belong to him; we are his people and he is our Master. As he obeyed the Father, so we obey him.

Jesus Christ is the exalted Lord. Someday all will acknowledge his lordship. He will be worshiped as Lord. He will receive the glory that he once laid aside when men and women who were once his enemies confess him as their Lord and Savior.

Jesus is Lord, the unique One, the Savior of sinners, the Master of his redeemed people, and the One who enjoys the eternal glory that is reserved for him alone.

Consider Philippians 2:5–11 in its entirety. Follow the line from the preexistence of Christ in the form of God, to his laying aside of his privileges in heaven, to his taking on humanity and the role of a servant, to his death on the cross and his resurrection from the dead, to his ascension and exaltation as Lord.

Now examine your life before him. Have you properly confessed Jesus as Lord? Does he maintain his proper place of lordship in your life? "Christ died and returned to life for this: that he might be Lord over both the dead and the living" (Rom. 14:9).

## —— Philippians 2:9–11 ——

For this reason God highly exalted him and gave him the name that is above every name, so that at the name of Jesus every knee will bow—in heaven and on earth and under the earth—and every tongue will confess that Jesus Christ is Lord, to the glory of God the Father.

## —— John 20:24–29 ——

But Thomas (called "Twin"), one of the Twelve, was not with them when Jesus came. So the other disciples were telling him, "We've seen the Lord!"

But he said to them, "If I don't see the mark of the nails in his hands, put my finger into the mark of the nails, and put my hand into his side, I will never believe."

A week later his disciples were indoors again, and Thomas was with them. Even though the doors were locked, Jesus came and stood among them and said, "Peace be with you."

Then he said to Thomas, "Put your finger here and look at my hands. Reach out your hand and put it into my side. Don't be faithless, but believe."

Thomas responded to him, "My Lord and my God!"

Jesus said, "Because you have seen me, you have believed. Blessed are those who have not seen and yet believe."

# The Confession

Thomas the disciple is known mostly for his doubt about the resurrection of Jesus. But by the grace of God, Thomas was led to make one of the greatest confessions about Jesus recorded in the Bible (John 20:24–29).

The other disciples told Thomas that they had seen the Lord alive. Thomas did not believe them and said he wouldn't unless he could see and touch Jesus for himself.

Eight days later, Jesus accommodated Thomas and allowed him to touch his wounds from the crucifixion. Thomas then said of Jesus, "My Lord and my God." Thomas is a believer.

God is leading men and women to the great confession of Jesus Christ as Lord, a confession that comes from a heart that believes in him. "If you confess with your mouth, 'Jesus is Lord,' and believe in your heart that God raised him from the dead, you will be saved. One believes with the heart, resulting in righteousness, and one confesses with the mouth, resulting in salvation" (Rom. 10:9–10).

We don't get resurrection appearances as the disciples did. We get the preaching of the Word of Christ, the good news! We get the proclamation that Christ died for our sins according to the Scriptures, that he was buried, and that he was raised on the third day according to the Scriptures (1 Cor. 15:3–4). This preaching comes in the power of the Holy Spirit to open closed minds and hearts to the truth and saving power of Christ's death and resurrection.

By the Word and Spirit, God is converting hearts from unbelief to faith in Jesus Christ. The real purpose of this converting work of God is that you and I and a massive throng of others will believe on the Lord Jesus Christ and be saved.

Believe today. And pray for unbelievers. Pray for the churches in your community to preach the gospel. Pray that hundreds, even thousands, of people in your city will repent of sin and believe in Jesus and make the great confession that he is Lord. Pray for these churches to be ready to help these new converts become growing disciples and faithful church members. Pray that a tangible expression of the kingdom of God will be made evident through the churches in your city. Pray that God would grant spiritual awakening, and bring many to a saving knowledge of himself.

## Ephesians 4:17–24

Therefore, I say this and testify in the Lord: You should no longer live as the Gentiles live, in the futility of their thoughts. They are darkened in their understanding, excluded from the life of God, because of the ignorance that is in them and because of the hardness of their hearts. They became callous and gave themselves over to promiscuity for the practice of every kind of impurity with a desire for more and more.

But that is not how you came to know Christ, assuming you heard about him and were taught by him, as the truth is in Jesus, to take off your former way of life, the old self that is corrupted by deceitful desires, to be renewed in the spirit of your minds, and to put on the new self, the one created according to God's likeness in righteousness and purity of the truth.

# Truth, Identity, and Jesus

We must, we are told, be who we are. We must identify ourselves by some designation that most closely aligns with our inner sense of self, and then be true to that identity in the way we live. We must "find our truth." The problem is, if we get our identity wrong at the beginning, the path we follow will also be wrong.

Ephesians 4 blows up the categories of identity that are so common among us. Here, the apostle Paul brings disruption to our "find your truth" thinking.

Paul commanded these Gentiles living in the first-century city of Ephesus to no longer live like Gentiles. He says Gentiles are confused and live in all kinds of sexual and relational confusion. They give expression to this confusion by practicing "every kind of impurity."

But these are Gentiles, so how can Paul tell them not to live like Gentiles? How is this not a violation of their personhood?

Our world would say the problem in Ephesians 4 is not with the Gentiles who are only being true to their "identity," but with Paul, who dares to tell them not to give expression to who they see themselves to be. The problem is that Paul is leading them to a form of internal damage to their sense of self by telling them not to do what they feel they must do.

Here's the disruption of the gospel. "Gentile" is not the fundamental identity of these Gentiles. People may be called Gentiles in the sense that they are not Jewish, and therefore represent the nations of the world. Though nationality and ethnicity are realities, they are not fundamental identities.

People are also called Gentiles in the sense that they were at one time outside of the promises of God and therefore living in spiritual darkness. But the Gentiles to whom Paul is writing have entered into the new life of Jesus Christ through repentance of sin and faith in him. They are now identified with the death and life of Jesus. They are "in Christ." The old person they were has died with Jesus on the cross, and they are now raised from the grave with him as new selves.

Jesus restores us to our true selves as God intended us to be. Through faith in Jesus, we join him in death to sin and newness of life. Our identity is summed up in these two words: "in Christ." Gentile, confused, darkened, ignorant, excluded, hard-hearted, promiscuous, impure, greedy, angry, dishonest, foul-mouthed, bitter, slandering, crude, and covetous (Eph. 4:18–5:4) is not who we are. We fight these and other sins that still want to rise up and express themselves, but they do not define who we are at the core of our being. Denying these sins will neither kill us nor violate our personhood. Sin is not our identity; we are "in Christ."

—— Acts 19:1–6 ——

While Apollos was in Corinth, Paul traveled
through the interior regions and came to Ephesus. He
found some disciples and asked them, "Did you receive
the Holy Spirit when you believed?"

"No," they told him, "we haven't even heard that
there is a Holy Spirit."

"Into what then were you baptized?" he asked them.

"Into John's baptism," they replied.

Paul said, "John baptized with a baptism of repentance, telling the people that they should believe in the
one who would come after him, that is, in Jesus."

When they heard this, they were baptized into the
name of the Lord Jesus. And when Paul had laid his
hands on them, the Holy Spirit came on them, and they
began to speak in other tongues and to prophesy.

# The Spirit of God

"The LORD is one," says the ancient statement of faith recited by Israel (Deut. 6:4). Yet, Jesus spoke of the three persons of God when he commanded his disciples to baptize believers in the name of the Father, Son, and Holy Spirit (Matt. 28:19). The Christian doctrine of the Trinity is a mystery affirmed in these passages and throughout the Bible. There is one God, he exists in three persons, each person is fully God, and yet God remains one. To know God, then, is to know him as Father, Son, and Holy Spirit.

Acts 19 records an account in the early years of the Christian faith, when the apostle Paul was evangelizing and planting churches throughout Asia Minor. Paul came across some disciples who knew only about John the Baptist's message of repentance, and had never heard about salvation in Jesus, nor received the Holy Spirit. These disciples received an education that day. After they learned about the Holy Spirit, they came to know God through his Spirit.

Do we know about the Holy Spirit? Many Christians, professing to believe in Jesus the Son of God, know very little about the Holy Spirit of God. Knowing little about the Spirit, they have little awareness of the Spirit's work in their lives.

To be a Christian, we must be born of the Holy Spirit. Once we are born again, we are to be filled with the Spirit by submitting to him. The filling of the Holy Spirit produces characteristics of Jesus in our lives called "fruit." The Bible is inspired by the Holy Spirit and as we read it, obey it, and make decisions by its wisdom, we are being led by the Spirit. The Holy Spirit creates fellowship among Christians. We serve others and share the gospel by the gifts and power that the Holy Spirit gives to us. These and other aspects of the nature and activity of the Holy Spirit are a part of any doctrine statement that is based on the Bible.

Now to the next question: Do we know God through personal experience with his Spirit? Have we received the Spirit through hearing the gospel with faith (Gal. 3:2)? Are we filled with the Spirit by submitting to him (Eph. 5:18)? Are we walking by the Spirit by following the path of his Word (Gal. 5:16)? Are we maintaining the unity of the Spirit in the bond of peace in relationship to other Christians in the context of a local church (Eph. 4:3)? Are we bearing the fruit of the Spirit by loving, serving, and reaching out to people with the gospel (Gal. 5:22)?

Receiving and responding to the truth about God's Spirit leads us to a deeper knowledge of God. Take some time to deepen your knowledge about the Holy Spirit, that you might know and honor him.

When the day of Pentecost had arrived, they were all together in one place. Suddenly a sound like that of a violent rushing wind came from heaven, and it filled the whole house where they were staying. They saw tongues like flames of fire that separated and rested on each one of them. Then they were all filled with the Holy Spirit and began to speak in different tongues, as the Spirit enabled them.

Now there were Jews staying in Jerusalem, devout people from every nation under heaven. . . . They were all astounded and perplexed, saying to one another, "What does this mean?" But some sneered and said, "They're drunk on new wine."

Peter stood up with the Eleven, raised his voice, and proclaimed to them: "Fellow Jews and all you residents of Jerusalem, let me explain this to you and pay attention to my words. For these people are not drunk, as you suppose, since it's only nine in the morning. On the contrary, this is what was spoken through the prophet Joel:

And it will be in the last days, says God, that I will pour out my Spirit on all people; then your sons and your daughters will prophesy, your young men will see visions and your old men will dream dreams. I will even pour out my Spirit on my servants in those days, both men and women and they will prophesy. I will display wonders in the heaven above and signs on the earth below: blood and fire and a cloud of smoke. The sun will be turned to darkness and the moon to blood before the great and glorious day of the Lord comes. Then everyone who calls on the name of the Lord will be saved.

# God's Spirit and God's People

Centuries before the Day of Pentecost, prophecies were made of the Spirit's coming on the church (Jer. 31:31; Ezek. 36:26; Joel 2:28–32). Jesus promised his disciples that after he left this earth the Father would send the Holy Spirit (Acts 1:8). And then it happened. On the Day of Pentecost, the new and gathered people of God "were all filled with the Holy Spirit" (Acts 2:4). A new relationship between God's Spirit and God's people began.

Of the many characteristics that mark God's people in the world, it is the filling of the Holy Spirit that lies beneath them all. Christians are born again, and that happens by the power of the Spirit. Love, joy, and peace are qualities of the Christian community, and it is the Holy Spirit who produces them in believers. The Word of God is the Spirit-inspired truth on which the people of God feed. The church is the witness of God's grace in the world. By the Spirit's power this witness goes forth.

*God's Spirit creates God's people through the miracle of the new birth.* "Blessed be the God and Father of our Lord Jesus Christ. Because of his great mercy he has given us new birth into a living hope through the resurrection of Jesus Christ from the dead" (1 Pet. 1:3). God's people are not just any people; they are new people. Are you walking in newness of life?

*God's Spirit indwells God's people and produces new qualities of life.* Jesus said, "I will ask the Father and he will give you another Counselor. . . . he remains with you and will be in you" (John 14:16–17). "The fruit of the Spirit is love, joy, peace, patience, kindness, goodness, faithfulness, gentleness, and self-control" (Gal. 5:22–23). God's people are different because the Holy Spirit is in them. Are the qualities of the Spirit being expressed from you to others?

*God's Spirit communicates to God's people with the truth he inspired.* "No prophecy of Scripture comes from the prophet's own interpretation . . . instead, men spoke from God as they were carried along by the Holy Spirit" (2 Pet. 1:20–21). When the church opens the Bible, the Spirit is communicating to you. Are you listening to the Spirit-inspired Word?

*God's Spirit empowers God's people to give testimony to the message of Christ.* This is the result of the Day of Pentecost. The people in Jerusalem that day each heard the declaration of the magnificent acts of God (Acts 2:11). God's Spirit moves God's people to speak of his greatness and grace. Is the gospel the message of your life?

Acts 2 shows us the created, indwelled, instructed, and empowered church gathered together in great joy. Renew your commitment to the people of God as you gather with your church in the fellowship of the Holy Spirit.

## Section II

# God's Work in Our Lives

—— GALATIANS 5:19–21 ——

Now the works of the flesh are obvious: sexual immorality, moral impurity, promiscuity, idolatry, sorcery, hatreds, strife, jealousy, outbursts of anger, selfish ambitions, dissensions, factions, envy, drunkenness, carousing, and anything similar. I am warning you about these things—as I warned you before—that those who practice such things will not inherit the kingdom of God.

—— ROMANS 3:23 ——

For all have sinned and fall short of the glory of God.

# The Weight of Sin Prepares Us for Christ

One of the most difficult sermons I have ever preached was from perhaps the most graphic and disturbing passage in the Bible, outside of the crucifixion of Jesus. In Judges 19–21, a woman is given up by her husband, in exchange for his own life, to a band of lustful men to be raped and abused. Here we see in narrative form what the New Testament puts in the form of propositions (Rom. 3:23; Gal. 5:19–21).

Often, we only have to turn on the television, open a browser on our computers, or read a newspaper to learn of equally graphic and disturbing events in our world. Abuse, murder, terrorist attacks, hate crimes—our world is filled with evil.

In the face of this, many will ask, "Where is God? Why does he let this kind of evil happen?" The book of Judges gives us the judgment, and it is not of God, but of us. This is the kind of thing that happens when, everyone does what is "right in his own eyes" (Judg. 21:25 ESV).

The weight of the sinful human condition needs to rest heavy on our consciences. This human condition is my condition and yours. We must resist our tendency to look for reasons for the evil in the world without looking at the sin in the human heart. While it can be emotionally crushing, admitting the sinfulness of the heart—of our own heart—is necessary.

Why? Because doing so prepares us for Christ. The last scene of Judges where a man offered up his concubine in exchange for his own life is a striking contrast to the scene of the cross where Christ offered up his own life in exchange for our freedom from the condemnation of sin.

We must know, feel, and acknowledge our sin before we will turn to Christ for salvation. We must turn to Christ for salvation before we will have freedom from our sin.

Look back to the passages above. Read again of the sins that we commit and the reality that no one is without sin. Let these difficult truths turn your eyes first to the state of your heart, then to Christ on the cross. Pray for the power of conviction and repentance that leads to life for yourself and for others who need to know the power of the gospel.

## Ruth 4:13–17

Boaz took Ruth and she became his wife. He slept with her, and the Lord granted conception to her, and she gave birth to a son. The women said to Naomi, "Blessed be the Lord, who has not left you without a family redeemer today. May his name become well known in Israel. He will renew your life and sustain you in your old age. Indeed, your daughter-in-law, who loves you and is better to you than seven sons, has given birth to him." Naomi took the child, placed him on her lap, and became his nanny. The neighbor women said, "A son has been born to Naomi," and they named him Obed. He was the father of Jesse, the father of David.

# Keep Reading

An accurate view of sin can leave us with a bleak picture of the human heart. When everyone does what is right in his own eyes, we all tend to do what is wrong in God's eyes—the sins of idolatry, abuse, greed, and disloyalty abound.

But tucked into the middle of the Bible, right after the horrible events at the end of Judges, is a short book called Ruth. It's a beautiful story of the Lord's gracious provision for two widows, of a woman and a man who treat each other with honor, and of a village of people who still love the Lord and their neighbors. One of the most striking aspects of the book of Ruth is that the opening line tells us that this kindness, faithfulness, honor, and loyalty took place, "during the time of the judges."

God gave us one book, Judges, to show us the depths of sin and what life is like when we do what is right in our own eyes. He gave us another book, Ruth, to show us his great faithfulness and what life can be like when we walk by faith in him.

Judges and Ruth together show us that we need to keep reading. We don't stop at the low points, the dark seasons, and the human depravity revealed in the Bible. We keep reading to find the high point of the cross of Christ, the light of the gospel of the glory of God in the face of Christ, and the power of the new creation for all who are in Christ.

On one level, we learn from reading these two books together that in our personal darkness we must keep looking for the light of God's faithfulness. He will provide. He will keep us. He will fulfill every promise he has made in his good and wise way. On another level, we learn something of God's plan of salvation. Judges ends on the horrible note of human sin, but Ruth ends on the hopeful note of God's grace. "Boaz fathered Obed, Obed fathered Jesse, and Jesse fathered David" (Ruth 4:21–22). Who was David? The righteous king who loved God and wrote the psalms and led his people to worship the Lord. But more importantly, it was his kingly line through which would come King Jesus, who saves us from our sin.

## Isaiah 7:14

"Therefore, the Lord himself will give you a sign: See, the virgin will conceive, have a son, and name him Immanuel."

## Isaiah 9:6

For a child will be born for us, a son will be given to us, and the government will be on his shoulders. He will be named Wonderful Counselor, Mighty God, Eternal Father, Prince of Peace.

# To Us a Son Has Been Given

The prophecy of Isaiah that a son would be given to us was made 735 years before Jesus' birth. After a long wait, Jesus was born. The Gospel of Matthew reaches back to Isaiah's prophecy to say that Jesus is the Son of promise (Matt. 1:21–23). From now on, we can say the Son *has been* given.

The Son that has been given is the center of the work God is doing in the world. It is clear to us as we read the Bible that we are to respond to him. Everything revolves around the Son, and his coming is the reality to be reckoned with. So, what do we do with Jesus? We should respond in at least three ways.

*Kiss the Son (worship).* "Pay homage to the Son" (Ps. 2:12). This means we are to give the Son the kiss of love and loyalty. We are called to worship.

*Conform to the Son (change).* "For those he foreknew he also predestined to be conformed to the image of his Son, so that he would be the firstborn among many brothers and sisters" (Rom. 8:29). This means we are to have our character conformed to that of Jesus. We are called to change.

*Keep up with the Son (serve).* "For even the Son of Man did not come to be served, but to serve, and to give his life as a ransom for many" (Mark 10:45). These words were spoken to the disciples as they lagged behind Jesus on the road to the cross. Jesus called the disciples to walk with him and keep pace with his purpose. We are called to serve.

As you consider the work God is doing in the world, respond to the call of the Son to worship, change, and serve.

## —— John 3:16–21 ——

"For God loved the world in this way: He gave his one and only Son, so that everyone who believes in him will not perish but have eternal life. For God did not send his Son into the world to condemn the world, but to save the world through him. Anyone who believes in him is not condemned, but anyone who does not believe is already condemned, because he has not believed in the name of the one and only Son of God. This is the judgment: The light has come into the world, and people loved darkness rather than the light because their deeds were evil. For everyone who does evil hates the light and avoids it, so that his deeds may not be exposed. But anyone who lives by the truth comes to the light, so that his works may be shown to be accomplished by God."

# Love Defined

In 1 John 2:15 we read, "Do not love the world or the things in the world. If anyone loves the world, the love of the Father is not in him." Now we read in John 3:16 that God loves the world. Shouldn't we love what God loves? Should we love the world, or not?

The answer is not found in redefining "world" by saying that we are not to love one kind of world while God loves another kind of world. The world is the world—in rebellion against God and under the judgment of God.

The answer is found in clearly defining love. The kind of love Christians are told not to have for the world is self-indulgent and participates in the self-exaltation of the world over the lordship of God. This kind of love for the world prefers things to God.

God's love is giving, sacrificing, and dying love. God's love provided the way of salvation in Christ and calls people in the world to repent, believe, and have life. God's love is the kind of love we are to have for the world.

What we need is the love of God to awaken in us love for God. The love of God for us and love for God in us will expel the wrong kind of love for the world. Then, we are in the position to rightly love the world.

Read the passage again. As you do, recognize that you need God's help to love him more, and to love the world like he loves the world. Ask God to work his love deep into your soul.

## ——— Acts 1:1–11 ———

I wrote the first narrative, Theophilus, about all that Jesus began to do and teach until the day he was taken up, after he had given instructions through the Holy Spirit to the apostles he had chosen. After he had suffered, he also presented himself alive to them by many convincing proofs, appearing to them over a period of forty days and speaking about the kingdom of God.

While he was with them, he commanded them not to leave Jerusalem, but to wait for the Father's promise. "Which," he said, "you have heard me speak about; for John baptized with water, but you will be baptized with the Holy Spirit in a few days."

So when they had come together, they asked him, "Lord, are you restoring the kingdom to Israel at this time?"

He said to them, "It is not for you to know times or periods that the Father has set by his own authority. But you will receive power when the Holy Spirit has come on you, and you will be my witnesses in Jerusalem, in all Judea and Samaria, and to the end of the earth."

After he had said this, he was taken up as they were watching, and a cloud took him out of their sight. While he was going, they were gazing into heaven, and suddenly two men in white clothes stood by them. They said, "Men of Galilee, why do you stand looking up into heaven? This same Jesus, who has been taken from you into heaven, will come in the same way that you have seen him going into heaven."

# Something Bigger Than Ourselves

No one would argue that we are not "selves," with possibilities and responsibilities. The Christian message affirms that we are individuals, accountable to God and called to follow Christ as such. As Christians, our new aim in life is to bring glory to God. This is our motivation for taking care of ourselves with food and clothing, physical protection, education, and income. We pursue relationships and work that give us a sense of fulfillment. We conduct ourselves appropriately when we interact with other people.

But being responsible selves is a much different thing than being locked into "self." Our human inclination is to be selfish. Selfishness is being all and only about "self." And that is a small world to live in. Nothing could be less interesting than the continual plodding around inside our own selves. Never leaving the narrow confines of self-interest restricts our humanness and limits our joy. That's the irony—the most appealing place to live is in our own world, but we soon realize it's a prison.

We need to be taken into something bigger than ourselves. We need a big story in which to find ourselves, a big purpose to motivate us, a big plan to pursue.

When Jesus said to deny ourselves, take up our cross, and follow him, he was calling us out of the small world of selfishness and into the bigger world of the kingdom of God. There is irony here, too. The most unappealing thing to do is to die to self, but doing so is a release from smallness that leads to a resurrection.

The book of Acts is a call out of smallness and into the bigger world of God's kingdom work. In Acts, individuals respond to Christ by faith and are gathered into the church. The church is caught up in the work of God's Spirit to extend the kingdom to the world. The whole plan of God for the world is laid out most clearly in the book of Acts. The gospel of the King and the kingdom goes to the end of the earth. The message of Acts is our salvation from smallness.

Consider today the smallness of self, and the enormity of the kingdom. As you do, pray that God would help you die to yourself. Pray that he would give you a glimpse of his kingdom. Pray also for the churches of your city and of the world, that they would be filled, not with individuals sold out for self, but individuals bought into the kingdom.

Peter stood up with the Eleven, raised his voice, and proclaimed to them: "Fellow Jews and all you residents of Jerusalem, let me explain this to you and pay attention to my words. For these people are not drunk, as you suppose, since it's only nine in the morning. On the contrary, this is what was spoken through the prophet Joel:

And it will be in the last days, says God, that I will pour out my Spirit on all people; then your sons and your daughters will prophesy, your young men will see visions, and your old men will dream dreams. I will even pour out my Spirit on my servants in those days, both men and women and they will prophesy. I will display wonders in the heaven above and signs on the earth below: blood and fire and a cloud of smoke. The sun will be turned to darkness and the moon to blood before the great and glorious day of the Lord comes. Then everyone who calls on the name of the Lord will be saved.

"Fellow Israelites, listen to these words: This Jesus of Nazareth was a man attested to you by God with miracles, wonders, and signs that God did among you through him, just as you yourselves know. Though he was delivered up according to God's determined plan and foreknowledge, you used lawless people to nail him to a cross and kill him. God raised him up, ending the pains of death, because it was not possible for him to be held by death. . . .

"God has raised this Jesus; we are all witnesses of this. Therefore, since he has been exalted to the right hand of God and has received from the Father the promised Holy Spirit, he has poured out what you both see and hear.

# The Holy Spirit and History

A good way to kill a party conversation is to tell someone you were a history major in college. People automatically assume you are into names, dates, and war facts, rather than music, sports, and good food.

While history may not be many people's favorite subject in school, no one can escape being a part of it. It's important to know the times in which we live, and how to live in them.

Acts 2 is a chapter in the Bible that tells us where we are in human history. Another term to use is "redemptive history." History is the activity of God governing and guiding the world, and drawing a people from the world to himself to be the church. That's what makes it redemptive.

In the sermon recorded in Acts 2, the apostle Peter begins with the words, "It will be in the last days." Peter is quoting the Old Testament prophet Joel, who said that a new day was coming. According to Peter, that day has come.

The "last days" are a new day in history, the days in which we live. What will be in these last days? What is happening in this era of history?

These are the days when Jesus Christ is acknowledged as both Lord and Christ. Peter traces the history of Jesus on earth and ends with his present place of authority in heaven to show us that he is Lord. Today, the news of Jesus is to spread to all the nations so he can be rightfully acknowledged as Lord.

These are the days when the Holy Spirit is poured out on the church in a new way. God's Spirit has always been active in the world and in the lives of his people. But after Jesus ascended into heaven, he poured out the Spirit in a new way. The Holy Spirit now fills God's people with new power to live new lives in a new community that gives witness to the defining reality that Jesus is Lord.

These days are a long day of opportunity for people to call upon the name of the Lord to be saved. Before Jesus returns, people will be saved and forgiven of sin and will receive the Holy Spirit through faith in him. Today is the day to repent and believe in Jesus and to identify with him and his people. Today is the day of salvation.

If these days are redemptive days, how then shall we live as the redeemed? Let us live under the lordship of Christ, filled with the Spirit of God, together making his name known in our cities and in our world, for the salvation of others.

—— Acts 2:36–41 ——

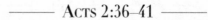

"Therefore let all the house of Israel know with certainty that God has made this Jesus, whom you crucified, both Lord and Messiah."

When they heard this, they were pierced to the heart and said to Peter and the rest of the apostles: "Brothers, what should we do?"

Peter replied, "Repent and be baptized, each of you, in the name of Jesus Christ for the forgiveness of your sins, and you will receive the gift of the Holy Spirit. For the promise is for you and for your children, and for all who are far off, as many as the Lord our God will call." With many other words he testified and strongly urged them, saying, "Be saved from this corrupt generation!" So those who accepted his message were baptized, and that day about three thousand people were added to them.

# The Holy Spirit and the Heart

In our day, there is little room in our lives for feeling bad. Taken to the extreme, this kind of thinking leaves no room for the work of the Holy Spirit in our hearts.

There is no virtue in self-loathing, shame, and sorrow over deeds when these things are ends in themselves. But when did we get the idea that the gospel leaves no room for the conviction of sin?

In Acts 2, after hearing a sermon on the lordship of Jesus and their guilt over killing him, the people were cut to the heart. The gift of the Holy Spirit in that moment was to convict their consciences. The Holy Spirit actually caused the internal pain of these people. In love, he afflicted them with a deep sense of remorse and regret. Fear came upon them as the Spirit exposed the intentions of their hearts and the sinfulness of their deeds.

Time spent with a guilty conscience is nearly unbearable. We want it gone and we want to relieve it in others. We soothe an unsettled conscience as quickly as possible. But we need to understand that being cut to the heart is a gift of the Holy Spirit and a necessary part of repentance that leads to life.

Peter was the designated preacher on the day these people were convicted of the sin of rejecting Christ. With contrition they asked him, "What shall we do?" Peter did not say, "Don't feel bad. God knows your hearts and he knows you're really good people." Nor did he say, "Too bad. What you've done is beyond forgiving." Rather, Peter knew that the Holy Spirit cut their hearts for a purpose. He knew that godly sorrow leads to repentance. He took full advantage of their contrition and told them to turn to the very one they had crucified by the hands of lawless men.

And they did.

The Spirit's work worked. Three thousand people received the message to repent of sin, were baptized to publicly identify with Jesus the Lord, and were added to the church. We then read that their sad hearts were filled with gladness, generosity, and praise to God.

Are you sensing the weight of sin and experiencing a growing sorrow of heart? Pay attention. The Holy Spirit is working. He is guiding you into repentance and into life in Christ. Reach out to another Christian who can talk to you about these things.

Are you praying for someone who has yet to be cut to the heart over sin? Pray for that very thing. In love, pray for conviction. Trust that God's Spirit is active when conviction happens, and when it does, respond by sharing the real remedy of repentance and faith in Christ.

## MATTHEW 1:18–25

The birth of Jesus Christ came about this way: After his mother Mary had been engaged to Joseph, it was discovered before they came together that she was pregnant from the Holy Spirit. So her husband Joseph, being a righteous man, and not wanting to disgrace her publicly, decided to divorce her secretly.

But after he had considered these things, an angel of the Lord appeared to him in a dream, saying, "Joseph, son of David, don't be afraid to take Mary as your wife, because what has been conceived in her is from the Holy Spirit. She will give birth to a son, and you are to name him Jesus, because he will save his people from their sins."

Now all this took place to fulfill what was spoken by the Lord through the prophet:

See, the virgin will become pregnant
and give birth to a son,
and they will name him Immanuel,
which is translated "God is with us."

When Joseph woke up, he did as the Lord's angel had commanded him. He married her but did not have sexual relations with her until she gave birth to a son. And he named him Jesus.

# Salvation: Private or Public?

"She will give birth to a son, and you are to name him Jesus, because he will save his people from their sins" (Matt. 1:21).

Jesus came to save his people from their sins. His people are *a people*, not just *individual people*. There is a corporate nature to salvation.

The testimony of the Bible is that God's purpose is to have a people who belong to him and he to them. This "people" is made up of people. Jesus saves people (individuals) to become his people (the church). Saved people and a saved church are the same purpose of God.

This brings up a question. Is our salvation personal, or is it private? We need to make the distinction. Salvation is personal. You and I, individually, must repent of sin and believe in Jesus Christ to be saved. No one can do this for us. Jesus calls us personally to deny ourselves, take up the cross, and follow him.

But salvation is not private. You and I are saved by grace through faith to become a part of the people of God. The people of God are individual Christians who make up the church of Jesus Christ.

There are massive implications to realizing that our faith in Christ is not private, and that we belong to something bigger than ourselves. We go to church with the expectation that God dwells among us. We together seek to live in devotion to Christ. We help one another and work together. We live together on mission in the world.

Personal faith is a must for salvation, but salvation is never a private experience. Jesus came to save his people from their sins.

Spend some time today thinking about salvation. Look for ways you may have privatized salvation by disconnecting from Christ's people, and ways you can experience and enjoy the corporate nature of salvation through the ministry of the church.

## Romans 1:8–15

First, I thank my God through Jesus Christ for all of you because the news of your faith is being reported in all the world. God is my witness, whom I serve with my spirit in telling the good news about his Son—that I constantly mention you, always asking in my prayers that if it is somehow in God's will, I may now at last succeed in coming to you. For I want very much to see you, so that I may impart to you some spiritual gift to strengthen you, that is, to be mutually encouraged by each other's faith, both yours and mine.

Now I don't want you to be unaware, brothers and sisters, that I often planned to come to you (but was prevented until now) in order that I might have a fruitful ministry among you, just as I have had among the rest of the Gentiles. I am obligated both to Greeks and barbarians, both to the wise and the foolish. So I am eager to preach the gospel to you also who are in Rome.

# Mercy and Transformation: God at Work in Us

These verses contain Paul's personal words to the Christians in Rome. In them we see God's work in Paul in two ways—showing him mercy and transforming his character.

The good news of the gospel includes God's willingness to rescue us from the horrible state of sin and self-centered destruction. Paul's story in Acts 9 and Philippians 3:5–6 shows us how a person can be religious but completely lost in sin, pursuing a path that harms others and will eventually result in damnation. Paul was trying to stop Christ! What a pitiful, sad, and serious state of being. What danger there is in being left to live a self-directed life! The end result is spiritual death.

God showed Paul mercy (1 Tim. 1:13). For Paul, God's mercy came in the form of physical blindness and then a vision to stop his murderous journey to Damascus. Jesus arrested Paul before he could bring further harm to people and condemnation upon himself. He made Paul his servant (Rom. 1:1). Jesus was not obligated to do this; he simply had mercy on a sinner.

Apart from the details, Paul's story is our story. Left to ourselves, we too will pursue the path that leads to death. But God shows us mercy in Christ Jesus. He stops us in our tracks, arrests us in our madness, and delivers us from the power of evil. God rescues us! This is mercy.

There is more. After Paul was shown mercy, we see him loving the very Christians he once wanted to kill. He is actually preaching to them and praying for them. He wanted to build their faith and was willing to risk his life to do so (Rom. 1:11). The only explanation for this transformation is God's mercy.

God will transform you. I have seen God turn mean people into great lovers. I have witnessed people consumed with lust become pure in heart. I have seen boldness in the timid, peace in the anxious, and generosity in the greedy. People have had their priorities so rearranged that their time, money, and desires are completely redirected. God transforms sinners so that they look more and more like saints.

If Paul were to appear to you today, he would tell you to throw yourself at the mercy of God. He would call you to repent of your sins and trust Jesus alone to make you right with God. He would show you how to come to God every day in repentance and faith to be renewed in your minds and redirected in your pursuits. He would tell you of the Spirit's work within you to make you aware of God's love and to make you more Christlike in character. If Paul were here, mercy and transformation would be his theme. Let it also be your theme.

--------- Mark 12:28–34 ---------

One of the scribes approached. When he heard them debating and saw that Jesus answered them well, he asked him, "Which command is the most important of all?"

Jesus answered, The most important is Listen, O Israel! The Lord our God, the Lord is one. Love the Lord your God with all your heart, with all your soul, with all your mind, and with all your strength. The second is, Love your neighbor as yourself. There is no other command greater than these."

Then the scribe said to him, "You are right, teacher. You have correctly said that he is one, and there is no one else except him. And to love him with all your heart, with all your understanding, and with all your strength, and to love your neighbor as yourself, is far more important than all the burnt offerings and sacrifices."

When Jesus saw that he answered wisely, he said to him, "You are not far from the kingdom of God." And no one dared to question him any longer.

# The Dynamic of the Gospel in the Heart

Discipleship is not dry duty, but the result of a spiritual dynamic at work in the heart of a person made new in Christ. This is seen clearly in the activity of love.

The command to love God and our neighbor is given, implied, or illustrated on every page of the New Testament. Jesus said the first and second most important commandments are to love God and to love our neighbor (Mark 12:28–34).

But the commands to love are not the sum of the gospel. The gospel is the love of God for us in Christ and the work of the Spirit in our hearts. God's love for us is the dynamic that produces the activity of our love for him and others.

God's love for us is most clearly seen in the fact that Jesus died for our sins. God's love for us is most powerfully communicated to us by the Holy Spirit who makes our hearts new and awakens us to him. God's love, in Christ and by the Spirit, is dynamic. It is a power that accomplishes salvation for us and produces responsiveness to God in us. Our energy to love God and our neighbor comes from the love of God for us.

To obey the command to love, we must first have the dynamic of the gospel at work in our hearts.

Receive the love of God for you in Christ. Christ died for your sin because you cannot remove the guilt of your sin on your own. Repent of your sin and trust in Christ for your salvation.

Renew your heart in the love of God for you in Christ. Open your Bible (Romans 8 is a great place to start) and let the Spirit of God communicate to you the deep love of God (Rom. 5:5). See the love of God for you in the cross of Christ (Rom. 5:8). Grasp the greatness of God's love for you (Rom. 8:31–39).

Respond from the heart to the love of God for you in Christ. Let the gospel become a power in you to love God and your neighbor. Let daily activities be done in love because God loves you.

Before the Passover Festival, Jesus knew that his hour had come to depart from this world to the Father. Having loved his own who were in the world, he loved them to the end.

Now when it was time for supper, the devil had already put it into the heart of Judas, Simon Iscariot's son, to betray him. Jesus knew that the Father had given everything into his hands, that he had come from God, and that he was going back to God. So he got up from supper, laid aside his outer clothing, took a towel, and tied it around himself. Next, he poured water into a basin and began to wash his disciples' feet and to dry them with the towel tied around him.

He came to Simon Peter, who asked him, "Lord, are you going to wash my feet?"

Jesus answered him, "What I'm doing you don't realize now, but afterward you will understand."

"You will never wash my feet," Peter said.

Jesus replied, "If I don't wash you, you have no part with me."

Simon Peter said to him, "Lord, not only my feet, but also my hands and my head."

"One who has bathed," Jesus told him, "doesn't need to wash anything except his feet, but he is completely clean. You are clean, but not all of you." For he knew who would betray him. This is why he said, "Not all of you are clean."

# Made Clean; Made New

"When God our Savior revealed his kindness and love, he saved us, not because of the righteous things we had done, but because of his mercy. He washed away our sins, giving us a new birth and new life through the Holy Spirit. He generously poured out the Spirit upon us through Jesus Christ our Savior." (Titus 3:4–6 NLT).

The death and resurrection of Jesus Christ provided for us the double blessing of being made clean and being made new.

Jesus died on the cross and was buried on a Friday. That death was in our place, to pay the penalty for our sins. By faith in him, we are forgiven. By being forgiven, we are made clean.

Jesus rose from the dead on a Sunday. That resurrection was for our life. His resurrection was a deathblow to death, showing that death no longer had controlling power over sinners because the One who died for sins had now come to life. By faith in him, the sinners for whose sins Jesus died are given the same life that Jesus now has. By faith, we are made new.

The death and resurrection of Jesus are made visible to us every time a Christian is baptized. A Christian's whole body is lowered into water as Jesus was put into the grave. The sins of this Christian are paid for and he is shown to be clean. A Christian is raised from the water as Jesus was raised from the dead. He is now shown to be raised with Jesus as a new person (Rom. 6:1–12).

Made clean and made new! This is the message of the gospel. Rejoice today that in Christ and because of Christ, you have been made clean and made new. Pray for someone you know who does not have a relationship with Christ. Ask God to draw that person to himself, so he or she can also be made clean and made new.

## 1 Corinthians 6:9–11

Don't you know that the unrighteous will not inherit God's kingdom? Do not be deceived: No sexually immoral people, idolaters, adulterers, or males who have sex with males, no thieves, greedy people, drunkards, verbally abusive people, or swindlers will inherit God's kingdom. And some of you used to be like this. But you were washed, you were sanctified, you were justified in the name of the Lord Jesus Christ and by the Spirit of our God.

# Gospel Change

The gospel is about God changing us. The gospel change described in 1 Corinthians 6:9–11 can be summed up in the phrase: Such you were, but now you are. Here Paul gives a list of the kinds of people who will not enter the kingdom of God. After the list is given, he says, "and some of you used to be like this."

Paul then says, "But you were washed, you were sanctified, you were justified." Now they are clean, set apart for God's purposes, forgiven, and made right with him. The Corinthian church was full of people who were changed by God's grace through faith in Jesus Christ. If you are a believer in Jesus, you too are clean, set apart, forgiven, and made right with God.

Change is a reality of the gospel, and it comes from God. The good news is that God reaches us as we are and makes us something new. He comes to us where we are and takes us somewhere else. "Such you were" describes us before gospel grace made the change. "Now you are" describes the change gospel grace makes.

Today, dwell on this passage from 1 Corinthians. Consider again what you were and what you now are by God's grace.

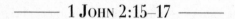

—— 1 JOHN 2:15–17 ——

Do not love the world or the things in the world. If anyone loves the world, the love of the Father is not in him. For everything in the world—the lust of the flesh, the lust of the eyes, and the pride in one's possessions—is not from the Father, but is from the world. And the world with its lust is passing away, but the one who does the will of God remains forever.

# A New Affection

"The love of the world cannot be expunged by a mere demonstration of the world's worthlessness. But may it not be supplanted by the love of that which is more worthy than itself? The heart cannot be prevailed upon to part with the world by a simple act of resignation. But may not the heart be prevailed upon to admit into its preference another, who shall subordinate the world, and bring it down from its wonted ascendancy? The only way to dispossess the heart of an old affection is by the expulsive power of a new one."[4]

The above quote is from a sermon preached in the early 1800s by Thomas Chalmers of Scotland called, "The Expulsive Power of a New Affection." The entire sermon is available on many websites. I encourage you to take the time and expend the mental energy to read it.

The sermon is based on 1 John 2:15: "Do not love the world or the things in the world. If anyone loves the world, the love of the Father is not in him."

Chalmers addresses the issue of how a person stops loving the world (meaning life and its pursuits apart from God). His main point is that a person does not stop loving the world simply by being told how bad the world is and then resolving to stop loving it. Chalmers says people can't just stop loving what they love and then be left without something else to love. That, he says, would go against how we are made, for we are made to set our love (our deepest affection) somewhere.

Chalmers preached that the way to stop loving the world is to have the love of God awaken in us a new and powerful affection. This new affection is for Christ. This new affection will become an expelling power, enabling and causing us to lose our love for the world.

And how does this new affection come to reside in our hearts? Chalmers says by putting before our minds the beauty and greater value of Jesus Christ as he is revealed in the gospel.

You and I will live by what we love. We will make our decisions, spend our time and energy, and pursue goals based on the deepest affection of our hearts. I encourage you to honestly evaluate what and who holds the affection of your heart. If it is not Jesus Christ, turn to him now and ask him to give you a new heart, and to fill it with love for him.

## HEBREWS 2:14–18

Now since the children have flesh and blood in common, Jesus also shared in these, so that through his death he might destroy the one holding the power of death—that is, the devil—and free those who were held in slavery all their lives by the fear of death. For it is clear that he does not reach out to help angels, but to help Abraham's offspring. Therefore, he had to be like his brothers and sisters in every way, so that he could become a merciful and faithful high priest in matters pertaining to God, to make atonement for the sins of the people. For since he himself has suffered when he was tempted, he is able to help those who are tempted.

# Fellowship with Jesus Our Lord

When I was a young Christian, I learned to meet with the Lord every day through reading my Bible and praying. This was called "fellowship" with God. Over the years I have tried to consistently do this in the mornings. I have benefited greatly from this practice.

But when 1 Corinthians 1:9 says, "God is faithful; you were called by him into fellowship with his Son, Jesus Christ our Lord," it is not referring to a time of Bible reading and prayer. Rather, it means God, by his grace, has called us to share in the life of Christ.

God awakens our souls to himself and his grace in the new birth. As new people with new hearts, the life of Christ is being formed in us (Gal. 4:19). We are being conformed to him (Rom. 8:29). Christ is in us (Col. 1:27). Christ abides in us, and we remain in him (John 15:4–5).

Fellowship with the Son, Jesus Christ our Lord, is more than a meeting with him to read and pray (though meeting with him is vital to fellowshipping with him). It is sharing, partaking of, and participating in his life.

So, when you meet with the Lord for Bible reading and prayer . . .

. . . remember that you are sharing in his life, he is in you, and you are in him.

. . . seek to conform your life (thinking, desiring, deciding) to him.

. . . take what you gain in that time with him into your experiences that day.

. . . rely upon his life in you, not your practice of time with him.

When God came near to us, he did so by sending his Son to become a man, that we, by faith, would have fellowship with him. Ask God to awaken your soul to the reality of the shared life of Christ.

## —— 2 Corinthians 12:1–10 ——

Boasting is necessary. It is not profitable, but I will move on to visions and revelations of the Lord. I know a man in Christ who was caught up to the third heaven fourteen years ago. Whether he was in the body or out of the body, I don't know; God knows. I know that this man—whether in the body or out of the body I don't know; God knows—was caught up into paradise and heard inexpressible words, which a human being is not allowed to speak. I will boast about this person, but not about myself, except of my weaknesses.

For if I want to boast, I wouldn't be a fool, because I would be telling the truth. But I will spare you, so that no one can credit me with something beyond what he sees in me or hears from me, especially because of the extraordinary revelations. Therefore, so that I would not exalt myself, a thorn in the flesh was given to me, a messenger of Satan to torment me so that I would not exalt myself. Concerning this, I pleaded with the Lord three times that it would leave me. But he said to me, "My grace is sufficient for you, for my power is perfected in weakness."

Therefore, I will most gladly boast all the more about my weaknesses, so that Christ's power may reside in me. So I take pleasure in weaknesses, insults, hardships, persecutions, and in difficulties, for the sake of Christ. For when I am weak, then I am strong.

# Comfort in Weakness

We usually have one of two responses to the experience of being weak. One is to ask God to remove the weakness. The other is to compensate for weakness with strength. What happens for the Christian when weakness simply will not go away?

The apostle Paul called his weakness a "thorn in the flesh" (2 Cor. 12:7). We don't know exactly what this thorn was, but we do know that it caused him enough pain, perplexity, and feelings of helplessness that he prayed three times for it to leave him. Perhaps one of the most sobering omissions in the Bible is a verse that says God took the thorn out of his flesh.

One of the most comforting verses in the Bible is the one that says Christ spoke to Paul in his weakness (not after he overcame). "My grace is sufficient for you, for my power is perfected in weakness" (2 Cor. 12:9). Comfort in unrelenting weakness is not found in a guarantee that it will be removed in this life or that we will overcome it with strength. Comfort is the promise of Christ's sustaining grace and his power in our weakness.

As you come face-to-face with various kinds of weaknesses, it is right to pray that God would remove them. But know that comfort does not come from him simply taking away your pain or struggles; comfort comes from the promise of Christ's grace. His power is made perfect in your weakness.

Jonah prayed to the LORD his God from the belly of the fish:

I called to the LORD in my distress, and he answered me.

I cried out for help from deep inside Sheol; you heard my voice. You threw me into the depths, into the heart of the seas, and the current overcame me. All your breakers and your billows swept over me. But I said, "I have been banished from your sight, yet I will look once more toward your holy temple. The water engulfed me up to the neck; the watery depths overcame me; seaweed was wrapped around my head. I sank to the foundations of the mountains, the earth's gates shut behind me forever! Then you raised my life from the Pit, LORD my God! As my life was fading away, I remembered the LORD, and my prayer came to you, to your holy temple. Those who cherish worthless idols abandon their faithful love, but as for me, I will sacrifice to you with a voice of thanksgiving. I will fulfill what I have vowed. Salvation belongs to the LORD."

Then the LORD commanded the fish, and it vomited Jonah onto dry land.

# Hope in the Belly of a Fish

The Lord commissioned the prophet Jonah to call out against the evil of the Ninevites. Jonah did not want to. So he went the other direction, as far from Nineveh and the presence of the Lord as he could (or so he thought). The Lord sent a great storm to threaten the ship Jonah boarded to flee from the Lord. Jonah was thrown overboard to save the ship and crew. Then God sent a great fish to swallow Jonah. Inside the fish, Jonah prayed to the Lord and determined to obey.

Many people question the part about the fish. They wonder how anyone could believe that a fish actually swallowed a man and that the man lived to pray another day. When I questioned this part of the Jonah account in my own mind, I remembered that the entire Christian faith is dependent on the resurrection of Jesus from the dead. If God can raise the dead, Jonah praying inside a fish is not such a stretch.

A bigger question than the reality of the fish is the purpose of the fish. The reason the Lord sent the fish to swallow Jonah was to rescue him from an otherwise certain death at the bottom of the sea. That rescue is a reason for hope. If you are ever running from the Lord and his call on your life, and he sends a fish to swallow you, there are four reasons you can be hopeful:

1. God is showing you that he has the power to fulfill his purposes and his plans, even if you are not entirely on board.
2. God is showing you that he is gracious enough to discipline you in order to rescue you from yourself.
3. God is showing you that he will not abandon you because his steadfast love endures forever.
4. God is giving you an opportunity to turn to him in prayer and repentance.

Thank God for his power, grace, and steadfast love, and for the opportunities he gives us, again and again, to turn to him in prayer and repentance.

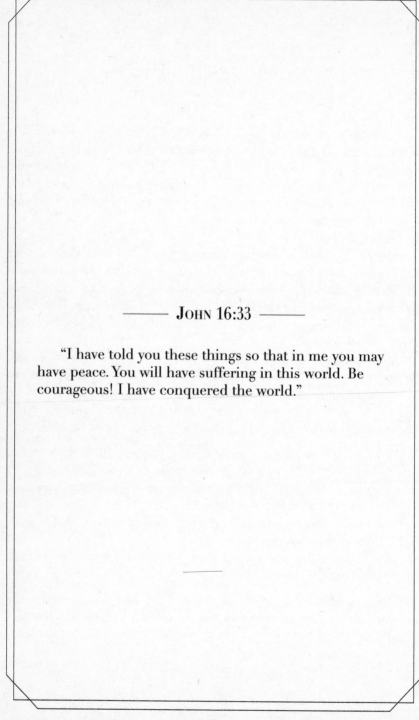

—— JOHN 16:33 ——

"I have told you these things so that in me you may have peace. You will have suffering in this world. Be courageous! I have conquered the world."

# A Future and a Hope

"Surely there is a future, and your hope will not be cut off" (Prov. 23:18 ESV).

I often pray for my congregation that we would see the future as God sees it and have hope.

Why this prayer? Because depression, anxiety, and other sorts of emotional and mental struggles are real. These things become spiritual struggles because they impact the way we relate to God. When the psalmist was in the midst of some kind of life struggle, he turned to God and said, "Why have you forgotten me?" (Ps. 42:9).

We all experience these struggles. It may be physical/chemical or circumstantial. Regardless, it causes us to ask God questions. That means it becomes a spiritual issue. And usually, the spiritual experience we have in the struggles of life is a faltering or loss of hope—we question the goodness of God and the future.

There are always many members of Christ's body living right at this point. And, when one member suffers, we all suffer. So will you pray for those who are suffering in your church?

Pray that they would see the future as God sees it and have hope. As Christians, our future includes the abiding presence of God, the ongoing work of God to make us like Jesus, and the eternal joys of God in heaven. As Christians, we have hope. Those who put their trust in him will never be put to shame (1 Pet. 2:6).

If you are in a difficult season, here are some practical ways to increase hope:

- Reach out.
- Make a phone call for help.
- Get out. Go to events and to church with helpful people.
- Serve. Do something to help someone else.
- Preach. Proverbs 23:18 is a one-sentence sermon. Take it, memorize it, pray it, quote it to yourself, and then give it away.

Jesus is our future. Jesus is our hope. Jesus will not disappoint.

## PHILIPPIANS 1:27

Just one thing: As citizens of heaven, live your life
worthy of the gospel of Christ. Then, whether I come
and see you or am absent, I will hear about you that
you are standing firm in one spirit, in one accord, contending together for the faith of the gospel.

# When "Strive" and "Gospel" Go Together

Paul called the Philippians to contend "together for the faith of the gospel." Other Bible translations use the verb "strive." This verse is one place when the words *strive* and *gospel* should be kept together.

We never strive in our own moral goodness to earn our salvation. "By grace through faith" is the gospel message. But we always strive for the faith of the gospel. To strive is to compete for a win. We strive for the faith of the gospel when we live so the gospel will win.

Let the gospel win in your heart. Trust completely and only in the work of Jesus for you on the cross. Don't trust in yourself. He is the only one who can forgive you and make you clean, and he will. Consider yourself spiritually alive because your Savior Jesus is alive in you. Remind yourself every day and every moment that you belong to Christ. Let this good news be a power in your heart that produces all kinds of goodness. Let love flow from you because the love of Christ has been set on you.

Let the gospel win in the Christian community. See the good news of Jesus as the main news of your church. Christians need the good news too, so share it with each other in your church. Relate to one another in a way that promotes love, joy, peace, patience, kindness, goodness, faithfulness, gentleness, and self-control. Pray that people who walk into your church service will be given good news.

Let the gospel win in your community. The gospel wins because God causes it to do so. God uses Christians and churches that are being changed by his grace to give testimony to his power and love. Some people from the community will respond to this testimony with faith. The gospel will win in their lives.

Let's pray and live for the gospel to win in our communities.

## ROMANS 8:1–4

Therefore, there is now no condemnation for those in Christ Jesus, because the law of the Spirit of life in Christ Jesus has set you free from the law of sin and death. What the law could not do since it was weakened by the flesh, God did. He condemned sin in the flesh by sending his own Son in the likeness of sinful flesh as a sin offering, in order that the law's requirement would be fulfilled in us who do not walk according to the flesh but according to the Spirit.

# The Power and Practicality
# of Not Being Condemned

The gospel declares that in Christ Jesus we are not condemned. Christ took on the penalty for our sins, thereby securing our pardon and forgiveness. Christ's righteous life was counted as ours, thereby securing our acceptance with God.

To be declared not condemned by God has massive implications for the way you live every day. Here are a few:

1. You have peace with God. You can live your life on this earth without being afraid of God. The Bible tells us to fear God, which means to respect, worship, listen to, and obey him. But as a Christian you are not to be afraid of God. In fact, Romans 8:15 tells you that you can call God, "*Abba*, Father."

2. You can fight the battle against sin with one less weight. Fighting against sin and temptation to sin is hard enough without carrying around guilt over the struggle. If you know that you are not condemned by God, a great weight is lifted and you gain new energy to focus on obedience to God from a heart of love.

3. You don't have to make up for past sins or maintain a perfect record before God. Your service to God and to others is motivated by love, which always makes the service sweeter.

4. You don't have to justify yourself to others. Imagine relating to others without being defensive. You are not condemned, and no one can condemn you before God, so when you interact with others you can focus on truth, love, and edification.

5. You will be less likely to judge and condemn others. As you understand the grace and mercy shown to you by God, you will begin to see others in light of their need of the same. Prayer and hope will replace judgment and condemnation.

6. You have entered a new relationship with God that makes you a partner with him in bringing truth, justice, mercy, and help to the world. "For God loved the world . . ." will become your motivation for living a life of influence in the world. The gospel will more naturally flow from you in word and deed.

God's truth is always powerful and practical. Pray today that your heart will be open as never before to the truth of Romans 8.

## ROMANS 12:1–8

Therefore, brothers and sisters, in view of the mercies of God, I urge you to present your bodies as a living sacrifice, holy and pleasing to God; this is your true worship. Do not be conformed to this age, but be transformed by the renewing of your mind, so that you may discern what is the good, pleasing, and perfect will of God.

For by the grace given to me, I tell everyone among you not to think of himself more highly than he should think. Instead, think sensibly, as God has distributed a measure of faith to each one. Now as we have many parts in one body, and all the parts do not have the same function, in the same way we who are many are one body in Christ and individually members of one another. According to the grace given to us, we have different gifts: If prophecy, use it according to the proportion of one's faith; if service, use it in service; if teaching, in teaching; if exhorting, in exhortation; giving, with generosity; leading, with diligence; showing mercy, with cheerfulness.

# Mercy among Us

The mercy by which God saves us and makes us his children, and by which we live for him with mind and body, also joins us to the church. The church is the experience of God's mercy among us.

Romans 12 shows us what it means for the church to live with God's mercy among us.

1. People who know God's mercy enter the church with humility. When we measure ourselves by the gospel standard of the cross of Christ, we see ourselves as recipients of grace. This spiritual sight leads to the expulsion of insane pride and sound judgment takes over. When humble people come to church, unity, service, and love abound.

2. People who know God's mercy contribute to unity in the church. Unity is not agreement on everything by everyone. Unity is the connection we have to one another that is rooted in the reality of salvation in Christ and expressed in the common confession that Jesus is Lord. Knowing that we belong to one another because we belong to Christ results in practical care for the church.

3. People who know God's mercy serve the church. God has given each person the ability to contribute to the church through service. Mercy and service are inseparable. Mentally and emotionally taking in the mercy of Christ for us on the cross provides the energy, initiative, and creativity needed to move toward others in service.

4. People who know God's mercy love the church. The greatest lovers are those who know they are loved. You are loved. The death of Christ for you is the demonstration of the love of God for you. The dynamic of gospel love is that it always flows outward to others.

"Mercy among us" is a great description of church life. We are in the church by mercy, we share God's mercy with each other, and we extend gospel mercy to the world. Let us keep a steady gaze on the cross to keep a steady flow of mercy among us.

## Ephesians 6:10–18

Finally, be strengthened by the Lord and by his vast strength. Put on the full armor of God so that you can stand against the schemes of the devil. For our struggle is not against flesh and blood, but against the rulers, against the authorities, against the cosmic powers of this darkness, against evil, spiritual forces in the heavens. For this reason take up the full armor of God, so that you may be able to resist in the evil day, and having prepared everything, to take your stand. Stand, therefore, with truth like a belt around your waist, righteousness like armor on your chest, and your feet sandaled with readiness for the gospel of peace. In every situation take up the shield of faith with which you can extinguish all the flaming arrows of the evil one. Take the helmet of salvation and the sword of the Spirit—which is the word of God. Pray at all times in the Spirit with every prayer and request, and stay alert with all perseverance and intercession for all the saints.

# The Power of Christ for the Church

The idea of power evokes strong feelings. For some, there is a reaction against power because its use is so often abusive and leaves people damaged. For others, there is a lust for power because it is seen as the way to gain control over people and security for themselves.

Power can get a bad reputation. But power is not inherently bad. It is the bad use of and the lust for power that leads to all kinds of evil.

Power is an important part of the Christian faith. We need a clear understanding of the kind of power that is Christ's, and how those "in Christ" are to use his power in our lives. Ephesians 6:10 tells Christians to be strong in the Lord's power. Two truths are given here. First, the Lord has power. Second, we are given his power as the strength to fight against the evil one.

Jesus Christ is Lord. God raised him from the dead and seated him at his right hand to have power and authority over all powers on earth and in heaven (Eph. 1:20–22). "All powers" includes the devil and evil spiritual beings, and the people and institutions of this world used by the devil to oppose Christ and to do harm. Jesus has power over them all.

Jesus was given as head over all things for the benefit of the church (Eph. 1:22). That means that the power of Christ is for the church to fight against the evil one. We are not given power to gain control over others, nor do we receive power to secure a comfortable world for ourselves. The power of Christ comes to the church to stand against the devil.

So how does the power of Christ come to the church? How are we strong in the Lord's strength? Ephesians 6:10–18 is the classic passage on the armor (strength and power) of God that comes to us "in Christ." The passage can be summarized to say that we receive the power of Christ in our lives through the grace of salvation, the walk of faith, the Word of God, and prayer in the Spirit. How we need to grow in this grace and in these graces!

Christ who is rich in power empowers his people. His power toward us who believe has made us alive with him to resist the devil and to serve people.

Are you being strengthened in the Lord's power today by his grace? Are you using his power to stand firm against the evil one and to serve others?

Today, meditate on the power that is yours in Christ.

## Ephesians 3:17–19

I pray that you, being rooted and firmly established in love, may be able to comprehend with all the saints what is the length and width, height and depth of God's love, and to know Christ's love that surpasses knowledge, so that you may be filled with all the fullness of God.

## Ephesians 5:1–2

Therefore, be imitators of God, as dearly loved children, and walk in love, as Christ also loved us and gave himself for us, a sacrificial and fragrant offering to God.

# Love Awakens Love

"Those who suppose that the doctrine of God's grace tends to encourage moral laxity . . . are simply showing that, in the most literal sense, they do not know what they are talking about. For love awakens love in return."[5]

That phrase, "love awakens love in return," is a major theme in the book of Ephesians. The apostle Paul is writing about the incalculable riches of Christ (Eph. 3:8). He prays that Christians will know the riches of Christ's love and how wide, and long, and high, and deep it is (Eph. 3:18). Then he calls Christians to walk in love (Eph. 5:1–2).

The flow of Paul's thought and of the Christian teaching of love is not hard to follow in Ephesians, or in the rest of the New Testament. God's love for us in Christ is immeasurable and unsearchable. As we come to know this love by grace through faith, our love is awakened. We come to love God with our whole selves, and to love our neighbor as ourselves (Matt. 22:37–40). We love because he first loved us (1 John 4:19). Knowing the riches of God's love for us in Christ is necessary to truly love God and others. Paul knew this, so he prayed for it (Eph. 3:14–19).

Love awakens love. So shouldn't knowing the love of God for us in Christ be our morning prayer (Ps. 143:8)? Our Bible study, preaching, and teaching should be to know this love. Christians should always be reminding each other of God's love for us. Our message to the world should be that, "God loved the world in this way: He gave his one and only Son, so that everyone who believes in him will not perish but have eternal life" (John 3:16).

Today, spend intentional time thinking about and rejoicing in the great love the Father has for you in Jesus his Son. Pray that the Holy Spirit will give you the eyes to see and the faith to embrace the rich love of God. Pray also that the Holy Spirit would start a great movement, bringing many who do not yet know the love of God to faith as they hear and embrace the gospel.

## JUDE 20–25

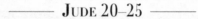

 But you, dear friends, as you build yourselves up in your most holy faith, praying in the Holy Spirit, keep yourselves in the love of God, waiting expectantly for the mercy of our Lord Jesus Christ for eternal life. Have mercy on those who waver; save others by snatching them from the fire; have mercy on others but with fear, hating even the garment defiled by the flesh.

 Now to him who is able to protect you from stumbling and to make you stand in the presence of his glory, without blemish and with great joy, to the only God our Savior, through Jesus Christ our Lord, be glory, majesty, power, and authority before all time, now and forever. Amen.

# Christ Will Keep Us

Here are my predictions for the next year: the church will be challenged and Christ will keep us in the love of God. These predictions are straight out of a small New Testament letter called Jude.

Jude is the book of the Bible that people jump over on their way to Revelation. It is basically a letter of warning. At the beginning, the writer, whose name is Jude, says he wanted to write an upbeat letter about the great salvation we share in Christ, but that he had to write a different kind of letter because some false teachers got in the church and started leading people into a less than holy lifestyle with their perverted teaching about grace (vv. 3–4). Jude says this is the very thing the apostles predicted would happen (v. 17).

The false teaching was a major challenge to the church. If the Christians listened to these grace-perverting teachers, they would be in danger of straying from the Christian faith.

Then, Jude makes another prediction in the form of a blessing. He gives praise to God who will keep the church from stumbling and falling into this false teaching (vv. 24–25). Jude shows great confidence in the keeping grace of Christ. Since Christ saves us by grace, he will also keep us by grace. He will lose none who are truly his.

From Jude, we can confidently say that we will continue to be challenged and tested in our faith as individual Christians and as the church. Even local congregations will find themselves dealing with teaching that doesn't square with the truth of the gospel and the kind of life that it produces in believers.

But we can also say that Christ will keep his people. *Jesus is and will be Lord of his church.*

There is one more thing we find in Jude that is important to keep in mind. We are given a very clear plan by which Christ will keep us. Jude calls us to build ourselves up in our faith and to pray in the Holy Spirit. We are to live steady and ready for the return of Christ. In this way we will keep ourselves in the love of God. We are to help each other stay in faith and the love of God by showing mercy.

The promise that Christ will keep us from stumbling and falling away from the faith doesn't mean that we do nothing to stay in the faith. That promise is the motivation we need to keep to the plan he has given us for faithfulness.

Consider today the challenges to your faith. What challenges is the enemy throwing your way? How is the world challenging your faith? What distorted versions of grace are you tempted to believe? Consider also the promise of Christ's keeping grace. Look to Jesus who promises to keep you, and commit to God's plan for staying faithful.

## Section III

# Responding to God in Faith

## Acts 11:15–18

"As I began to speak, the Holy Spirit came down on them, just as on us at the beginning. I remembered the word of the Lord, how he said, 'John baptized with water, but you will be baptized with the Holy Spirit.' If, then, God gave them the same gift that he also gave to us when we believed in the Lord Jesus Christ, how could I possibly hinder God?"

When they heard this they became silent. And they glorified God, saying, "So then, God has given repentance resulting in life even to the Gentiles."

# Repentance That Leads to Life

Perhaps one of the most compact and clear statements of the grace of God toward us is found in Acts 11:18, "So then, God has given repentance resulting in life even to the Gentiles." The early leaders of the Christian church, who were all Jewish, made that statement.

These leaders had just heard how Peter, the leader among leaders, preached the gospel to a Gentile (non-Jewish) man named Cornelius. Cornelius, along with other Gentiles with him, received and believed the gospel, and were given the gift of the Holy Spirit. The movement in their hearts toward Christ was called repentance. Repentance means to turn. They turned to Christ. This turn led to life. How are we to understand the repentance that leads to life?

God grants the repentance that leads to life. The early Jewish leaders of the Christian church realized that people do not turn to Jesus on their own. They understood that repentance is a human response that happens as the Spirit of God works in many ways to turn people to Christ. When they saw Gentiles for the first time turning to Christ, they could not refute the fact that God had done this. So they simply rejoiced. Are you rejoicing today that God has granted you repentance that leads to life?

The repentance that leads to life is for all kinds of people. Gentile? Yes! Those who these Jewish leaders would previously not eat with are now being welcomed into the church of Jesus Christ. Your nationality, race, previous behavior, lack or abundance of prior religious experience or personal goodness, or any other quality about you makes no difference in repentance. God grants this gift to all kinds of people and all people must repent from all things to turn to Christ. Are you rejoicing today that nothing about you prevents God from granting you the repentance that leads to life?

The repentance that leads to life is for salvation. This is a controversial point of the gospel. Salvation requires repentance. Turning to Jesus in faith to follow him is the only way a person is saved. Do you hear this call to repent and believe in Jesus?

The repentance that leads to life is the way of discipleship. This is a misunderstood point of the gospel. Discipleship requires ongoing repentance. Yes, we repent and believe to be saved, but our ongoing growth in Christlikeness requires that we continue to turn from our self-life to follow him. Are you living close enough to Jesus that you are hearing how to repent on a daily basis?

Repentance leads to life. In repentance we are being turned from the death that results from sin to the life that is ours through forgiveness of sin. We are made alive to God. We live with Jesus now and forever.

## GALATIANS 6:11–14

Look at what large letters I use as I write to you in my own handwriting. Those who want to make a good impression in the flesh are the ones who would compel you to be circumcised—but only to avoid being persecuted for the cross of Christ. For even the circumcised don't keep the law themselves, and yet they want you to be circumcised in order to boast about your flesh. But as for me, I will never boast about anything except the cross of our Lord Jesus Christ. The world has been crucified to me through the cross, and I to the world.

# Authentic Christianity

The New Testament letter called Galatians was written by the apostle Paul to the churches in Galatia. It is a very important letter, and as with any correspondence, the last words are significant. We want to pay close attention to the final words of this letter. In his last sentences, Paul sums up the essence of authentic Christianity.

The many voices and variations within the Christian community today can make it difficult to find the main message of the gospel. I can imagine the confusion a person trying to understand the Christian faith in our culture might have.

The new Christian can also be confused after hearing and believing the message of the gospel and then attending a church with its practices and programs. Which ones are essential to following Jesus, and which ones are not? This is the challenge of discipleship.

Even people who have been Christians for a long time can lose sight of the essence of the faith. The activities associated with discipleship and church life can distract us from the heart of the gospel.

What is authentic Christianity? The closing words of Galatians tell us. Authentic Christianity is the message of the death of Jesus Christ on the cross for our sins. This message was given to the apostles who transmitted it to us in the form of Scripture. Authentic Christianity includes the inward transformation of people through the new birth in Christ. Those who are forgiven of their sins and born again by the power of God are now the people of God who live under the blessings of peace and mercy.

Authentic Christianity is to be the theme of the Christian life. I pray that the final words of Galatians will be helpful to you in your understanding of the gospel and your desire to live by its power.

The beginning of the gospel of Jesus Christ, the
Son of God. As it is written in Isaiah the prophet:
See, I am sending my messenger ahead of you;
he will prepare your way.
A voice of one crying out in the wilderness:
Prepare the way for the Lord;
make his paths straight!
John came baptizing in the wilderness and proclaiming a baptism of repentance for the forgiveness of
sins. The whole Judean countryside and all the people
of Jerusalem were going out to him, and they were
baptized by him in the Jordan River, confessing their
sins. John wore a camel-hair garment with a leather
belt around his waist and ate locusts and wild honey.
He proclaimed, "One who is more powerful than I am
is coming after me. I am not worthy to stoop down and
untie the strap of his sandals. I baptize you with water,
but he will baptize you with the Holy Spirit."

In those days Jesus came from Nazareth in Galilee
and was baptized in the Jordan by John. As soon as
he came up out of the water, he saw the heavens being
torn open and the Spirit descending on him like a
dove. And a voice came from heaven: "You are my
beloved Son; with you I am well-pleased."

Immediately the Spirit drove him into the wilderness. He was in the wilderness forty days, being
tempted by Satan. He was with the wild animals, and
the angels were serving him.

After John was arrested, Jesus went to Galilee, proclaiming the good news of God: "The time is fulfilled,
and the kingdom of God has come near. Repent and
believe the good news!"

# Following Jesus

The Gospel of Mark in the New Testament transports us back to the beginning of the good news about and from Jesus. In these verses, we encounter Jesus Christ, the Son of God. We see him in action—healing, overcoming evil, and performing signs that verify his message. We hear his teaching and his call to individuals to follow him. We watch these people respond and become his followers. This short gospel is packed with Jesus' power, call, and response.

Reading Mark is one of the most personal and life-altering things we can do. When Jesus calls Simon, James, John, Levi, and the crowd of people around him to follow him, we hear Jesus calling us. The words of Jesus come off the page and become the voice that resonates in our ears and quickens our hearts. Jesus' voice is alive and relevant. Jesus' call changes everything.

I believe the greatest need for every individual, every family, every neighborhood, every city, and every country is to hear the call of Jesus to follow him. Mark says Jesus came into Galilee proclaiming the gospel of God. When we open the Bible, Jesus comes into your home, your heart, and your mind, proclaiming this good news.

Consider again the call of Jesus to discipleship from the Gospel of Mark. Think about those in your life who are not following Jesus, and who need to hear this most important call. Pray for them today, and consider inviting them to read the Gospel of Mark with you, that Jesus might come proclaiming the gospel to them.

There was a man from the hill country of Ephraim named Micah. He said to his mother, "The 1,100 pieces of silver taken from you, and that I heard you place a curse on—here's the silver. I took it."

Then his mother said, "My son, may you be blessed by the LORD!"

He returned the 1,100 pieces of silver to his mother, and his mother said, "I personally consecrate the silver to the Lord for my son's benefit to make a carved image and a silver idol. I will give it back to you." So he returned the silver to his mother, and she took five pounds of silver and gave it to a silversmith. He made it into a carved image and a silver idol, and it was in Micah's house.

This man Micah had a shrine, and he made an ephod and household idols, and installed one of his sons to be his priest. In those days there was no king in Israel; everyone did whatever seemed right to him.

# True Worshipers

Worship is the expression of the relationship of grace and faith that we have with God. This relationship (called a covenant in the Bible) is foundational. God calls, saves, keeps, and leads us by grace. We respond to him in faith. Faith is trust, love, and obedience. Worship is the expression of this relationship in various aspects.

When the relationship between grace and faith breaks down, so does worship. We see this clearly in Judges 17. The nation of Israel had forgotten the grace of God, grown cold in love for him, abandoned his commands, and taken on the ways of the surrounding Canaanite culture. The next thing we see is the practice of worship so corrupted with paganism that it could no longer be called worship at all. The evil practices of using idols, setting up private places of worship in disobedience to God's commands, and employing clergy who give worshipers what they want in exchange for money is evidence of covenant unfaithfulness.

Judges 17 is a warning. The warning is about our hearts in worship and how we worship. But it is in Jesus, not in Judges, where we find the corrective.

Jesus said in John 4 that God is seeking worshipers who worship him in Spirit and truth. These worshipers have drunk deeply from the grace of God and are indwelt by the life-giving Spirit. They have come to the Truth, who is Jesus Christ. True worshipers of God have hearts made clean and new and worship the Father, in the Spirit, through the Son.

With clean and new hearts, true worshipers come to God the way he instructs. They come with humility, gratitude, adoration and devotion. True worshipers listen to God with a readiness to obey. They worship God in his way, revealed by his Word.

One troubling temptation I've noticed over the years is to approach the Sunday gathering for worship as an event to attend rather than an expression of a relationship. Let's heed the warning of Judges. Let's hear the call of Jesus to come to the Father who has called us by grace. Let our worship be the obedience of faith that will keep the worship event unmixed with the idols of a selfish heart. Let us guard our hearts so our worship will be pure.

Pray that the power of the Spirit and the Word would hold sway over your own heart, and over your church, as you worship individually and corporately.

For you have not come to what could be touched, to a blazing fire, to darkness, gloom, and storm, to the blast of a trumpet, and the sound of words. Those who heard it begged that not another word be spoken to them, for they could not bear what was commanded: If even an animal touches the mountain, it must be stoned. The appearance was so terrifying that Moses said, I am trembling with fear. Instead, you have come to Mount Zion, to the city of the living God (the heavenly Jerusalem), to myriads of angels, a festive gathering, to the assembly of the firstborn whose names have been written in heaven, to a Judge, who is God of all, to the spirits of righteous people made perfect, and to Jesus, the mediator of a new covenant, and to the sprinkled blood, which says better things than the blood of Abel.

See to it that you do not reject the one who speaks. For if they did not escape when they rejected him who warned them on earth, even less will we if we turn away from him who warns us from heaven. His voice shook the earth at that time, but now he has promised, Yet once more I will shake not only the earth but also the heavens. This expression, "Yet once more," indicates the removal of what can be shaken—that is, created things—so that what is not shaken might remain. Therefore, since we are receiving a kingdom that cannot be shaken, let us be thankful. By it, we may serve God acceptably, with reverence and awe, for our God is a consuming fire.

# Let Us Worship

We often view the worship of God as an event that we attend on Sundays. But there is a greater reality to our worship than what we do during the worship service.

We worship God because Jesus brought us to God. God himself has sent out the Word that both warns and invites. His Word warns us of judgment to come for the unbelieving and invites us to be reconciled to him by believing in his Son. Through Jesus we have come to the living God, to his city, to his family, to worship him.

This great gospel reality is the basis of our worship and the reason for our worship, and it shapes our attitude when we worship. Gathering for the worship service with the local congregation is a priority for those who are running the race of enduring faith in Jesus. But corporate worship is not an end in itself; it glorifies God by making visible the good news that he has reconciled us to himself.

Hebrews 12:18–29 is about worshiping God because he has called us to himself, and we have come to him by faith in Jesus. Think on these things throughout your day, and give thanks to God who has called you to himself by his Son Jesus. Make gathering with your congregation for worship a priority in your life. And pray that the gospel of Jesus will be clearly communicated and embraced by faith in your church.

## PHILIPPIANS 3:17–4:1

Join in imitating me, brothers and sisters, and pay careful attention to those who live according to the example you have in us. For I have often told you, and now say again with tears, that many live as enemies of the cross of Christ. Their end is destruction; their god is their stomach; their glory is in their shame. They are focused on earthly things, but our citizenship is in heaven, and we eagerly wait for a Savior from there, the Lord Jesus Christ. He will transform the body of our humble condition into the likeness of his glorious body, by the power that enables him to subject everything to himself.

So then, my dearly loved and longed for brothers and sisters, my joy and crown, in this manner stand firm in the Lord, dear friends.

# Where to Set Our Affection

One big temptation we face as Christians is to set our affection on earthly things and to forget about the things of heaven. We feel the tension of living in two worlds the moment we read about this temptation in Philippians 3. We are not yet in heaven; we live on this earth, so we must think about things we know to be temporary. How then can we not set our affections here?

Several times in the New Testament we are told not to set our mind on earthly things, but on heavenly things. The word *mind* is used to refer to something deeper than just a thought. It means our affection, our love, our primary concern. Certainly we give thought to the things of this world. In fact, I am giving thought to the meal I will eat after I finish writing this. We pay attention to our schedules, our bank accounts, and our relationships. But that is different from thinking of these things as being the lasting and ultimate end of our lives. We can eat, sleep, and make money without making a god of our bellies, beds, or bank accounts. We can attend to the things on earth without worshiping them (Phil. 3:19).

How can we do this? By knowing the truth of our true citizenship. We belong, first and foremost, to heaven, from where we await the return of our Savior, the Lord Jesus Christ (Phil. 3:20). Because we belong to heaven first, we seek first the kingdom of God (Matt. 6:33). Since we have been raised up with Christ, we seek the things above, where he is. We set our affection on things that are above and not on things that are on earth (Col. 3:1–2).

Tension. That's what we feel. But this tension must be felt if we are to know that we are living faithfully as citizens of heaven who are pilgrims on this earth.

As you live today, don't try to resolve the tension. Let the tension be your reminder that you live here tending to your busyness with joy and faithfulness, but that you belong to heaven where your ultimate investment and hope lie. Let the knowledge of your heavenly citizenship prioritize what you give your life to and how you give it. Let the things of the kingdom of heaven impact the things you do on earth. Go be creative in your heavenly calling to glorify God in all things.

## ROMANS 8:9–14

You, however, are not in the flesh, but in the Spirit, if indeed the Spirit of God lives in you. If anyone does not have the Spirit of Christ, he does not belong to him. Now if Christ is in you, the body is dead because of sin, but the Spirit gives life because of righteousness. And if the Spirit of him who raised Jesus from the dead lives in you, then he who raised Christ from the dead will also bring your mortal bodies to life through his Spirit who lives in you.

So then, brothers and sisters, we are not obligated to the flesh to live according to the flesh, because if you live according to the flesh, you are going to die. But if by the Spirit you put to death the deeds of the body, you will live. For all those led by God's Spirit are God's sons.

# The Spirit Leads Us to Kill Sin

Romans 8:9–14 tells us that if we belong to Christ, we have his Spirit. If we have the Spirit, our spirit is alive and our mortal bodies will be given life. With that as the foundation, we are then told that by the Spirit we are to put to death the sins of the body.

We are led by the Spirit to kill sin and we must follow the Spirit in killing sin. Each time we exercise our faith and act against sin and for holiness, we are following the Spirit's lead.

Here are eight actions you can take to follow the Spirit's lead to kill sin and to greatly enjoy God.

1. Be aware of the principle of sin (Rom. 7:14–25). There is a war going on inside every Christian. We are God's children and filled with God's Spirit, but in our humanness we still struggle against our tendency toward sin and selfishness. Don't be surprised by the battle within.

2. Be aware of your sin. We are tempted in a variety of ways, but each person usually has a few areas of struggle that are more intense than others. Know yourself and be on guard for the particular ways you are stirred up to sin. Doing so will help you fight for faithfulness.

3. Humble yourself before God. Don't deny or ignore the presence of sin. Don't blame others for your sin. Open your heart and admit your sin to God. Submit to his searching Word and Spirit and repent of the sin that is revealed to you.

4. Rely upon the Spirit to deal with the sins of the heart, and work toward dealing with the sins of the heart.

5. Meditate on the cross of Christ. Seeing the Savior on the cross elevates in our minds the sinfulness of sin and the graciousness of Christ.

6. Develop your affection for Christ. Love for Christ is the greatest power for expelling sin from our lives. Think often of the character and love of Jesus revealed in Scripture.

7. Live in spiritual fellowship with others. Talk and pray with friends who can help you and keep you accountable for your life.

8. Persevere. Romans 8:13 says we are to be killing sin. That means we will be killing sin the rest of our lives. Keep going to God for grace through the Spirit and the Word.

Remember that the purpose of being led by the Spirit to kill sin is to more fully enjoy and glorify God. Keep God as your greatest end!

It is actually reported that there is sexual immorality among you, and the kind of sexual immorality that is not even tolerated among the Gentiles—a man is sleeping with his father's wife. And you are arrogant! Shouldn't you be filled with grief and remove from your congregation the one who did this? Even though I am absent in the body, I am present in spirit. As one who is present with you in this way, I have already pronounced judgment on the one who has been doing such a thing. When you are assembled in the name of our Lord Jesus, and I am with you in spirit, with the power of our Lord Jesus, hand that one over to Satan for the destruction of the flesh, so that his spirit may be saved in the day of the Lord. Your boasting is not good. Don't you know that a little leaven leavens the whole batch of dough? Clean out the old leaven so that you may be a new unleavened batch, as indeed you are. For Christ our Passover lamb has been sacrificed. Therefore, let us observe the feast, not with old leaven or with the leaven of malice and evil, but with the unleavened bread of sincerity and truth.

I wrote to you in a letter not to associate with sexually immoral people. I did not mean the immoral people of this world or the greedy and swindlers or idolaters; otherwise you would have to leave the world. But actually, I wrote you not to associate with anyone who claims to be a brother or sister and is sexually immoral or greedy, an idolater or verbally abusive, a drunkard or a swindler. Do not even eat with such a person. For what business is it of mine to judge outsiders? Don't you judge those who are inside? God judges outsiders. Remove the evil person from among you.

# A Theology of Suffering to Fight Sin
# and Be Faithful to Jesus

We hold martyrs in high regard. Laying down one's life for Jesus' sake is in our minds the highest form of self-denial. But are there not other forms of suffering for Jesus' sake? Does not Jesus call each of us to "deny [yourself], take up [your] cross daily, and follow me" (Luke 9:23)?

We need a theology of suffering that includes more than physical death. Our theology of suffering must include living with the pain of deliberately chosen unfilled desires for the sake of fighting sin and being faithful to Jesus. When our desires are sinful, we are called to suffer the death of them.

In 1 Corinthians 5 we find a man who had a sinful desire to participate in sexually immoral behavior. This man claimed to be a Christian and was a member of the church in Corinth. He thought that acting on his sinful desire was consistent with his profession of faith in Jesus, and that having his sinful desire left unfulfilled was inconsistent with his view of God and grace. He could not imagine that God would call him to die to what he wanted even when what he wanted was contrary to God's will. He did not have a theology of suffering that included death to his sinful desires for the sake of faithfulness to Jesus.

Would God really call us to live with unfulfilled desires? Certainly! He loves us enough to tell us to die to sinful desires because they are contrary to his will and will kill our souls.

Is there any good that can come from suffering the death of sinful desires? Absolutely! Jesus meets us in this kind of suffering. We come to know him and things about him that we would not know if we indulge our sinful desires. Suffering the death of sinful desires in submission to Jesus leads to fellowship with him that is so deep that those previously held desires are nothing in comparison. When we enter the joy of the kingdom of God, we will not feel as if we have been deprived.

Brother, sister, we do not have to have everything we naturally want. We will not die if our sinful desires are put to death. We will not be less than whole people if we kill the part of us that is in rebellion against God. Quite the opposite: "If by the Spirit you put to death the deeds of the body, you will live" (Rom. 8:13).

Some are called to die physical deaths for the sake of Jesus. All are called to die deaths to sinful desires for the sake of Jesus. There is no exception for anyone who would follow him. There is no greater joy than fellowship with Jesus in whatever kind of suffering we endure for his sake.

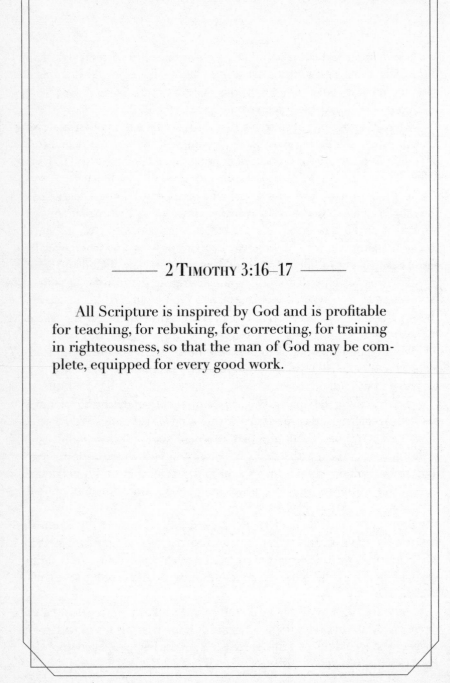

###### 2 TIMOTHY 3:16–17

All Scripture is inspired by God and is profitable for teaching, for rebuking, for correcting, for training in righteousness, so that the man of God may be complete, equipped for every good work.

# The Holy Spirit and Scripture

"What God has joined together, let no one separate" (Matt. 19:6). Jesus was talking about marriage when he spoke these words, but they also apply to the Holy Spirit and Scripture.

Too often, Christians think that the ministry of the Holy Spirit is unrelated to Scripture. We create two categories in our minds. One is for the work of the Holy Spirit. This, we think, is the realm of subjectivity, of feelings and promptings that come to us by the Spirit to show us what to do in a given moment. The other category is for the Scriptures. This category, we think, is using the mind to study written words that are going to be a challenge to obey. We tend to keep the Holy Spirit and the Scripture in two separate mental spaces. These categories are neither helpful nor accurate.

All throughout the Scripture itself we see that its inspiration, fulfillment, and ongoing accomplishment is because of the work of the Holy Spirit. The Holy Spirit inspired the men who wrote Scripture (2 Tim. 3:16; 2 Pet. 1:20–21). What the Holy Spirit spoke through those who wrote the Scriptures must be fulfilled (Luke 24:44). And the work of the Holy Spirit in the human heart leads to obedience to the Scriptures (Ezek. 36:27). The work of the Holy Spirit is for the recording, obeying, and fulfilling of the Word of God.

We find this conjoined ministry of the Holy Spirit and accomplishment of Scripture in the first chapter of Acts. The apostles understand that what was written in the Psalms was spoken by the Holy Spirit. And we see them acting in ways that, through their obedience, will accomplish what was written in the Psalms. The apostles also understand that the Holy Spirit spoke what is in Scripture and led them to accomplish what is written in Scripture. They were not willing to separate the work of God's Spirit from obedience to God's Word.

In addition to the Scripture from 2 Timothy, read the first chapter of Acts today. Learn from the apostles and their understanding of the work of the Holy Spirit and the Holy Scriptures.

"Everything is permissible for me," but not everything is beneficial. "Everything is permissible for me," but I will not be mastered by anything. "Food is for the stomach and the stomach for food," and God will do away with both of them. However, the body is not for sexual immorality but for the Lord, and the Lord for the body. God raised up the Lord and will also raise us up by his power. Don't you know that your bodies are a part of Christ's body? So should I take a part of Christ's body and make it part of a prostitute? Absolutely not! Don't you know that anyone joined to a prostitute is one body with her? For Scripture says, The two will become one flesh. But anyone joined to the Lord is one spirit with him.

Flee sexual immorality! Every other sin a person commits is outside the body, but the person who is sexually immoral sins against his own body. Don't you know that your body is a temple of the Holy Spirit who is in you, whom you have from God? You are not your own, for you were bought at a price. So glorify God with your body.

# Glorify God with Your Body

The Christian's body is the temple of the Holy Spirit. Our bodies were bought with the price of Christ's blood. Our bodies will be raised in newness when Christ returns. Our bodies belong to God, so we are called to glorify God with our bodies.

How we glorify God with our bodies contains some mystery. One clear way to do this is to flee from sexual immorality and pursue love in the use of our bodies. This is the specific issue being addressed by the apostle Paul to the Corinthian church.

When it comes to the proper use of the physical body in relation to sexual activity, the Bible gives us both negative and positive commands. In 1 Corinthians 6 the command is to put a stop to the use of the body to engage in sexual immorality, and to flee from this sin. The positive command is to use the body for the Lord's service, and to glorify him with it.

Romans 6 is helpful in the same way. Here we find a negative and a positive command—both of which are very practical. First, Paul gives a theological rationale for the good use of the body. He says that by faith in Christ we have union with him. That's a theological way of saying that what is true of Christ is true of us. Christ died for our sins, so we die to sin. Christ was raised from the grave, so we are new people and will be raised someday with him. These bodies are for the Lord and will be raised by him.

Since this is true, we are called to "offer" all the parts of our bodies to God for obedience to him and in service to him. Another way of saying this is that we are to make an offering to God each day and to give him every part of our bodies. Hands, feet, brains, and sexual organs all belong to God, and are to be daily presented to him for obedience. That means we follow God's commands with what we do and don't do with our body parts.

Think about how you can begin each day making an offering of every part of your body to the Lord for his glory and the good of others. What difference would that make in what you think, say, see, hear, and do throughout the day?

Now in response to the matters you wrote about: "It is good for a man not to use a woman for sex." But because sexual immorality is so common, each man should have sexual relations with his own wife, and each woman should have sexual relations with her own husband. A husband should fulfill his marital duty to his wife, and likewise a wife to her husband. A wife does not have the right over her own body, but her husband does. In the same way, a husband does not have the right over his own body, but his wife does. Do not deprive one another—except when you agree for a time, to devote yourselves to prayer. Then come together again; otherwise, Satan may tempt you because of your lack of self-control. I say this as a concession, not as a command. I wish that all people were as I am. But each has his own gift from God, one person has this gift, another has that.

I say to the unmarried and to widows: It is good for them if they remain as I am. But if they do not have self-control, they should marry, since it is better to marry than to burn with desire.

To the married I give this command—not I, but the Lord—a wife is not to leave her husband. But if she does leave, she must remain unmarried or be reconciled to her husband—and a husband is not to divorce his wife. But I (not the Lord) say to the rest: If any brother has an unbelieving wife and she is willing to live with him, he must not divorce her. Also, if any woman has an unbelieving husband and he is willing to live with her, she must not divorce her husband. For the unbelieving husband is made holy by the wife, and the unbelieving wife is made holy by the husband.

# Glorify God in Your Marriage

In 1 Corinthians 7, the apostle Paul naturally moves to a discussion of marriage as a continuation of his teaching on sexual purity in 1 Corinthians 6. This is because sexual purity and sexual immorality necessarily have to do with marriage. And that is because sexual activity was created for and only for the context of marriage.

Paul's teaching on marriage reveals that while God is glorified in our bodies as we keep them sexually pure, he is also glorified in our marriages as we use our bodies for sex. Sexual expression in marriage is a form of sexual purity, as sex was created for the context of marriage.

This topic is important because it is central to our witness of the wisdom of God. As Christians communicate that God's wisdom warns people against sexual immorality (sex outside of the context of heterosexual marriage), we also communicate that God's wisdom encourages and blesses sex in marriage.

When a husband and wife join together in sexual activity, they are doing more than enjoying physical pleasure; they are enjoying covenant love. They are also communicating the nature of that love. By reserving sex for their marriage to one another, they are expressing love that is exclusive, committed, self-giving, protected, cherished, honored, and enjoyed. These are the qualities of the love that exists between God and his people. God's people are to live with pure devotion to him.

Does this mean that Christians who are not married cannot reflect the nature of covenant love? Not at all. Sexual abstinence in obedience to Christ is a statement of faith. To obey God regarding the proper context for sex says loud and clear that one knows and believes that the greatest pleasure in this life, and in the next one, is undistracted devotion and unhindered fellowship with Christ.

We are not just preaching morality when we talk about God's wisdom in the use of sex. We are pointing to God: his creation, design, wisdom, and grace to forgive us for going our own way, restoring us to a life that brings glory to him.

—— 1 CORINTHIANS 7:17–24 ——

Let each one live his life in the situation the Lord
assigned when God called him. This is what I command in all the churches. Was anyone already circumcised when he was called? He should not undo his
circumcision. Was anyone called while uncircumcised?
He should not get circumcised. Circumcision does not
matter and uncircumcision does not matter. Keeping
God's commands is what matters. Let each of you
remain in the situation in which he was called. Were
you called while a slave? Don't let it concern you. But
if you can become free, by all means take the opportunity. For he who is called by the Lord as a slave is the
Lord's freedman. Likewise he who is called as a free
man is Christ's slave. You were bought at a price; do
not become slaves of people. Brothers and sisters, each
person is to remain with God in the situation in which
he was called.

# Glorify God in Your Calling

One question many Christians ask is, "Am I doing what I am supposed to be doing in life?" One confusion many Christians have is thinking the most important thing in life is what we do.

It seems this was the question and the confusion Paul dealt with in the church at Corinth. These Christians thought they must change something about their station in life in order to live out their calling before God. Paul assured them that as long as what they were doing in life was not sinful, they did not need to make a change. In fact, he told them to remain in their current station in life and to walk with God in it. In this way, they would find many opportunities to bring glory to God.

To the Jews and Greeks in the Corinthian church who were concerned about their ethnic status, Paul said what matters most is being born again and giving evidence of new life by keeping God's commandments. To the bondservants in the church who were concerned about their social and economic status, Paul said to change it if they could, but to remember that they were already free in Christ. Christ had called them, so wherever they were in life was the place of their calling.

The most important thing in life is not what we do, or even what our status is ethnically, socially, or economically. The most important thing in life is what Jesus has done for us and, therefore, what we have become in him.

When the good news of what Jesus has done for us and the new identity he has given us sink deep into our souls, we live wherever we are, doing whatever we do, with a deep commitment to obey him and a deep desire to reflect his glory. Walk confidently today where God has already called you.

## PHILIPPIANS 2:12–16

Therefore, my dear friends, just as you have always obeyed, so now, not only in my presence but even more in my absence, work out your own salvation with fear and trembling. For it is God who is working in you both to will and to work according to his good purpose. Do everything without grumbling and arguing, so that you may be blameless and pure, children of God who are faultless in a crooked and perverted generation, among whom you shine like stars in the world, by holding firm to the word of life. Then I can boast in the day of Christ that I didn't run or labor for nothing.

# New Obedience

Jesus said, "If you love me you will keep my commands" (John 14:15). The apostle Paul echoed this statement when he said, ". . . work out your own salvation . . ." (Phil. 2:12). To work out our salvation is to keep the commandments of our Savior.

Obedience is a priority for Christians. We do not work *for* our salvation. No amount of obedience to Bible commands changes our nature or atones for our sins. By grace we are saved through faith. But as the ones who have received grace, and who now walk by faith, obedience to God becomes our new desire and way of living. Obedience is working *out* our salvation, which is our discipleship.

We need to give more attention to obedience to Christ. The direct commands of the Bible are to be heeded. Commandments like "don't murder, steal, commit adultery, and lie" still direct our behavior, not just because some of these things are illegal, but also because they grieve our Lord. Commandments like "honor your parents, serve each other, worship God, and seek first his kingdom" still govern our lives as his people.

We can be thoughtful and creative in our obedience. The neighbor we are commanded to love can be our spouse, coworker, the person who lives next door, and people we don't even know. We can love these people in a thousand different ways according to the need of the moment and what we have to offer them. We can love them by doing things that would be helpful or honoring to them, and by not doing things that would be unhelpful or dishonoring to them.

Working out our salvation in obedience to Christ is not working for our salvation in legalism. We don't need to become overly scrupulous for fear of not attaining our salvation. It is God who works in us to save us, creates the desire for obedience, and gives us the power to live for his pleasure. Our obedience is living by his power and under his direction.

Today, how will you work out your salvation in some form of obedience to Christ?

——— PHILIPPIANS 2:12–18 ———

Therefore, my dear friends, just as you have always obeyed, so now, not only in my presence but even more in my absence, work out your own salvation with fear and trembling. For it is God who is working in you both to will and to work according to his good purpose. Do everything without grumbling and arguing, so that you may be blameless and pure, children of God who are faultless in a crooked and perverted generation, among whom you shine like stars in the world, by holding firm to the word of life. Then I can boast in the day of Christ that I didn't run or labor for nothing. But even if I am poured out as a drink offering on the sacrificial service of your faith, I am glad and rejoice with all of you. In the same way you should also be glad and rejoice with me.

# Creative Obedience

Yesterday, we saw in Philippians 2:12–16 that "working out our salvation" is essentially the obedience to Christ that comes with new birth of the Spirit. This is exactly what was prophesied in the Old Testament. "I will give you a new heart and put a new spirit within you. . . . I will place my Spirit within you, and cause you to follow my statutes" (Ezek. 36:26–27).

We also saw that we are called to be creative in our obedience. Many people see their obedience to God similarly to that of a child being scolded or coerced by a parent to obey. The child reaches for something he shouldn't touch and the parent thumps his fingers to keep him away. Or the child doesn't want to do what she should and the parent stays on her until she finally follows through. That's not what I would call creative obedience.

Others see obedience as merely doing direct commands and not doing directly forbidden things. This approach to obedience is narrow and does the bare minimum that is required. Again, this is not very creative, nor does it flow from a joyful heart.

But as new people in Christ we have a new way of thinking about obedience to God. When we hear Jesus command us to love our neighbor, we start looking for ways to do it. These ways may not be directly mentioned in the Bible, but they are stirred up in our imagination because the Bible is in our thinking. When we are told that the Holy Spirit lives in us and we are to glorify God with our bodies, we joyfully yield our bodies to God each day and look for ways to use them for service rather than for sin. The command to seek first the kingdom of God is for us an open door to all manner of gospel advance.

Creative thinking from the new desires and with the new deciding power of the new birth makes obedience a joy.

## 1 CORINTHIANS 7:29–31

This is what I mean, brothers and sisters: The time is limited, so from now on those who have wives should be as though they had none, those who weep as though they did not weep, those who rejoice as though they did not rejoice, those who buy as though they didn't own anything, and those who use the world as though they did not make full use of it. For this world in its current form is passing away.

# A Radical Question for Every Christian

What is radical discipleship? Some think if it's big, out of the ordinary, and dangerous, it's radical. Some think "radical" is only for a few, and the rest of us are just average. Not true on both accounts.

In 1 Corinthians 7, the apostle Paul gives us a radical way of doing ordinary life as followers of Christ. He tells us that discipleship is making decisions about every aspect of our lives based on devotion to Christ. Whether we are married, single, experiencing the sorrow or joys of life, or doing business, the main question to ask is how we can be undivided in our love and service to Christ. That is radical.

Discipleship is doing everyday things in a radically different way than we would if we did not know Jesus. Discipleship is participating in all of life as if nothing in this life is our ultimate goal. Discipleship is holding everything in this life with an open hand because we cannot hold on to it forever. Discipleship is seeking first the kingdom of God in our current station in life.

Radical discipleship is a new way of living in the ordinariness of life, and it is for every Christian.

How do we live this way? First, by the power of the gospel that changes us from the inside out. New vision, new desires, new aspirations, and new loves must grow in our hearts by the increasing awareness that in Christ we have all things.

Second, by thinking. It takes a lot of mental engagement and creativity to live fully engaged in the world with undivided devotion to Christ.

Pray today about what it means for you to be an ordinary radical Christian.

## 1 Corinthians 10:1–13

Now I do not want you to be unaware, brothers and sisters, that our ancestors were all under the cloud, all passed through the sea, and all were baptized into Moses in the cloud and in the sea. They all ate the same spiritual food, and all drank the same spiritual drink. For they drank from the spiritual rock that followed them, and that rock was Christ. Nevertheless God was not pleased with most of them, since they were struck down in the wilderness.

Now these things took place as examples for us, so that we will not desire evil things as they did. Don't become idolaters as some of them were; as it is written, The people sat down to eat and drink, and got up to party. Let us not commit sexual immorality as some of them did, and in a single day twenty-three thousand people died. Let us not test Christ as some of them did and were destroyed by snakes. And don't complain as some of them did, and were killed by the destroyer. These things happened to them as examples, and they were written for our instruction, on whom the ends of the ages have come. So, whoever thinks he stands must be careful not to fall. No temptation has come upon you except what is common to humanity. But God is faithful; he will not allow you to be tempted beyond what you are able, but with the temptation he will also provide a way out so that you may be able to bear it.

# Our Exodus in Temptation

We are promised that with every temptation we face, God is faithful to provide a way of escape (1 Cor. 10:13). The way of escape is not a way that avoids the temptation, but a way through it and a way to endure it.

Temptation is a given for every follower of Jesus. We won't be beyond temptation until we are beyond this life. The way of escape in every temptation is ever present. Jesus is that way.

When Paul talks about our temptations in 1 Corinthians 10, he uses the temptation God's people faced during the Exodus as the example of failure. They got out of Egypt (the place of bondage and oppression), but because of their sin, most of them did not get into the Promised Land.

The Gospel of Luke tells us that Jesus fulfilled his exodus (departure from this world) in Jerusalem where he died on the cross (Luke 9:31). Since the cross was for our sin and our salvation, Jesus also fulfilled our exodus.

Jesus is our exodus, our way of escape. He is our way out of sin by redeeming us from it. When we are tempted to sin, we can remember that Jesus died to deliver us from it.

Jesus is our way through temptation by suffering it with us. In our temptations we can talk to him and draw strength from him because he is with us.

Jesus is our way into God's glory by bringing us into right relation with him. When we are tempted to sin, we can cast our vision to the glory that awaits us and away from the sin that so easily entangles us. No wonder we are told to look "to Jesus, the founder and perfecter of our faith" (Heb. 12:2 esv).

Remember today as you inevitably face temptation that Jesus is the way of escape.

## 1 Corinthians 9:24–27

Don't you know that the runners in a stadium all race, but only one receives the prize? Run in such a way to win the prize. Now everyone who competes exercises self-control in everything. They do it to receive a perishable crown, but we an imperishable crown. So I do not run like one who runs aimlessly or box like one beating the air. Instead, I discipline my body and bring it under strict control, so that after preaching to others, I myself will not be disqualified.

# Self-Discipline or Legalism?

I have heard Christians use the word *legalism* when they have discussions about self-discipline. There seems to be confusion about what legalism is.

Legalism is depending on our efforts to secure and maintain right standing with God. We become legalists when we fail to grasp the reality of God's grace that grants us salvation by faith and not by works.

Once we are saved by God's grace through faith in Jesus Christ, we are called to exercise self-control and practice discipline in order to live a life in keeping with our salvation. We do not practice self-discipline to get or keep ourselves saved. We do it to live in keeping with salvation. The motive behind self-discipline is important. If it is for salvation, it is legalism. If it is from salvation, and in keeping with salvation, it is discipleship.

Both discipline and legalism have to do with the glory of God. Discipline that flows from our new life in Christ is for the purpose of bringing glory to God. Legalism that seeks to obtain right standing with God by works actually competes with the glory of God's grace.

Consider today, based on this passage from 1 Corinthians, the relationship between self-discipline and the glory of God. Are you pressing on, not to earn your salvation by works, but to glorify God in your obedience to him?

## Philippians 2:1-11

If then there is any encouragement in Christ, if any consolation of love, if any fellowship with the Spirit, if any affection and mercy, make my joy complete by thinking the same way, having the same love, united in spirit, intent on one purpose. Do nothing out of selfish ambition or conceit, but in humility consider others as more important than yourselves. Everyone should look out not only for his own interests, but also for the interests of others.

Adopt the same attitude as that of Christ Jesus, who, existing in the form of God, did not consider equality with God as something to be exploited. Instead he emptied himself by assuming the form of a servant, taking on the likeness of humanity. And when he had come as a man, he humbled himself by becoming obedient to the point of death—even to death on a cross. For this reason God highly exalted him and gave him the name that is above every name, so that at the name of Jesus every knee will bow—in heaven and on earth and under the earth—and every tongue will confess that Jesus Christ is Lord, to the glory of God the Father.

# Humility

As Christians we let Jesus set our priorities. He tells us what we should be like and what we should pursue. He does so in the Bible.

When we read the Bible, we notice that some of the things we think are so important are just not there. And some of the things we deem irrelevant or impractical for our modern age are on nearly every page.

Humility is one of those things that is central to being a follower of Christ, but to which many of us pay little attention. Philippians 2:1–11 is one of the greatest statements in the Bible about humility, and about the nature and work of Jesus Christ. It tells us that Jesus was humble.

Jesus humbly came to earth as a man, became a servant, and obeyed the will of the Father all the way to the cross. The humble Christ died for our sins to save us from the wrath of God and an eternity in hell.

But what we fail to realize is that the very reason this passage was written is to call for *our* humility. If you read closely, you see that Christ's humility is given as an example to us, showing us how to live before God and others. Why have we missed this point? Because while we like Christ's humility, we don't want to practice it ourselves.

Here's the good news about humility: When we live humbly before God, we live in fellowship with Christ. Without the nearness of Christ in humility, we should all avoid it as much as possible. But God took notice of the humility of his Son, Jesus, and he takes notice of his humble sons and daughters. To be with Christ and cared for by God is a strong motivation to humble ourselves before him.

Read this passage again, this time as a conversation with Christ. What does it reveal about his humility? Where do you need to embrace the mind of Christ, and imitate him?

## Romans 12:9–21

Let love be without hypocrisy. Detest evil; cling to what is good. Love one another deeply as brothers and sisters. Outdo one another in showing honor. Do not lack diligence in zeal; be fervent in the Spirit; serve the Lord. Rejoice in hope; be patient in affliction; be persistent in prayer. Share with the saints in their needs; pursue hospitality. Bless those who persecute you; bless and do not curse. Rejoice with those who rejoice; weep with those who weep. Live in harmony with one another. Do not be proud; instead, associate with the humble. Do not be wise in your own estimation. Do not repay anyone evil for evil. Give careful thought to do what is honorable in everyone's eyes. If possible, as far as it depends on you, live at peace with everyone. Friends, do not avenge yourselves; instead, leave room for God's wrath, because it is written, Vengeance belongs to me; I will repay, says the Lord. But

If your enemy is hungry, feed him.

If he is thirsty, give him something to drink.

For in so doing

you will be heaping fiery coals on his head.

Do not be conquered by evil, but conquer evil with good.

# Humble Love

Our estimation of ourselves is rooted in pride. We're human, which means a pre-occupation with self is in our nature. This obsession with self is pride. It colors the way we see everything.

Have you ever wondered why you struggle with thinking either too lowly or too highly of yourself? Have you figured out that the problem is the same whether it's too low or too high—it's simply thinking about yourself too much!

One big problem with this kind of thinking is that when it's about us, it can't be about others. When our pride causes us to be obsessed with ourselves, we are not good lovers of people.

The gospel tells us how to think of ourselves according to God's estimation. God sees things the way they really are. The cross of Christ reveals the way God sees things. The cross pulls back the curtain on the realities of God's holiness and wrath against our sin. Yet it is the cross that demonstrates God's love for sinners. The cross tells of the undeserved nature of our salvation, for there Jesus did for us what we could not do for ourselves. Jesus died for our sins.

The effect of seeing ourselves in light of the cross is that we are humbled. We see the depth of love Jesus has for us and the depth of sin from which he delivered us. We see that we didn't earn or deserve our salvation. There is simply no room left for pride in our hearts.

The humbled person is not preoccupied with self, but is occupied with Christ. Being occupied with Christ and thinking on him is actually the best way to be free from the prideful self-consciousness. Humbled by the cross, and freed from self-obsession, we are now in a position to love.

Bow before the cross in prayer. Get up in humility. Go love someone.

## —— Hebrews 11:8–16 ——

By faith Abraham, when he was called, obeyed and set out for a place that he was going to receive as an inheritance. He went out, even though he did not know where he was going. By faith he stayed as a foreigner in the land of promise, living in tents as did Isaac and Jacob, coheirs of the same promise. For he was looking forward to the city that has foundations, whose architect and builder is God.

By faith even Sarah herself, when she was unable to have children, received power to conceive offspring, even though she was past the age, since she considered that the one who had promised was faithful. Therefore, from one man—in fact, from one as good as dead—came offspring as numerous as the stars of the sky and as innumerable as the grains of sand along the seashore.

These all died in faith, although they had not received the things that were promised. But they saw them from a distance, greeted them, and confessed that they were foreigners and temporary residents on the earth. Now those who say such things make it clear that they are seeking a homeland. If they were thinking about where they came from, they would have had an opportunity to return. But they now desire a better place—a heavenly one. Therefore, God is not ashamed to be called their God, for he has prepared a city for them.

# Abraham and Sarah's Faith

Abraham and Sarah are presented to us in Hebrews 11 as examples of faith. But when you read the account of their lives in Genesis 12–21, they look, like the rest of us, like examples of stumbling, bumbling humans.

So what do their lives teach us about faith?

They do not teach us that faith knows all the details of God's plan, for God let them live in ambiguity for a long time.

They do not teach us that faith always makes the best judgment calls in the real situations of life, for they certainly had their share of difficulty due to decisions they made.

They do not teach us that faith ignores the limitations of being human, for they saw themselves as way too old to have a baby, even though God said they would.

They do, however, teach us that faith considers God—the One who made the promise—to be faithful. That kind of faith keeps us going even when we don't know the details, make some bad decisions, and see our own limitations.

God has promised a salvation that is both now and not yet. He will be faithful to his promise. We, like Abraham and Sarah, are called to live and die in faith. Walk in that faith today.

—— HEBREWS 11:17–19 ——

By faith Abraham, when he was tested, offered up
Isaac. He received the promises and yet he was offering his one and only son, the one to whom it had been
said, Your offspring will be called through Isaac. He
considered God to be able even to raise someone from
the dead; therefore, he received him back, figuratively
speaking.

# Abraham's Faith and Obedience

Yesterday, we saw the faith of Abraham and Sarah. Though faithful people still make mistakes, as Abraham and Sarah made evident, we must be clear that faith *does* lead to obedience.

According to Hebrews 11:17, Abraham's faith was tested when God told him to offer his son Isaac as a burnt offering (a sacrifice). You will want to read the account in Genesis 22. Each time I read this passage, I can feel the tension in my chest.

Abraham was enabled to obey God because he considered God able to raise Isaac from the dead. This short, simple statement of faith explains Abraham's obedience. Abraham did not bother himself with defending God's reputation because he believed God could raise up what Abraham offered up. Rather than worry about what other people might think of God for giving the command that he did, Abraham obeyed the command and let God take care of himself.

Abraham did not make the apparent dilemma of God his problem. As New Testament scholar F. F. Bruce points out, the dilemma of the Genesis account is reconciling the promise of God to bring about a nation of people through Isaac with the command of God to sacrifice Isaac.[6] Yet, Abraham treated this as God's problem, not his. Abraham's job was simply to obey. And he did obey, because he considered God able to solve the dilemma by raising Isaac from the dead.

Abraham did not fear for his own well-being. He trusted God to take care of him. Abraham's assurance was wrapped up in his son. Not only was Isaac Abraham's child, but he was proof of the promise God made to Abraham. But Abraham knew that God was able to make good on his promise—even if it meant raising Isaac from the dead.

Very often we live less than obedient lives because we think we have to defend God for some of his "radical" commands, or solve apparent contradictions between God's commands and promises, or simply take care of ourselves.

Abraham shows us how to live a life of obedience to God rooted in a belief that God is able.

## Hebrews 12:1–3

Therefore, since we also have such a large cloud of witnesses surrounding us, let us lay aside every hindrance and the sin that so easily ensnares us. Let us run with endurance the race that lies before us, keeping our eyes on Jesus, the source and perfecter of our faith. For the joy that lay before him, he endured the cross, despising the shame, and sat down at the right hand of the throne of God.

For consider him who endured such hostility from sinners against himself, so that you won't grow weary and give up.

# How Will We Be Faithful?

How?

We have been asking that question all of our lives. From tying our shoes to solving a math problem to navigating the adult world of career, family, and finances, we need to know how to do it.

The author of Hebrews compares the life of faith to a race. Being faithful to Jesus is compared to running the race with endurance. Hebrews 12:1–3 shows us how to do just that.

First, we have to define the race. Following Jesus by faith now and all the way to heaven is the race before us.

Second, we have to lay aside the sin that keeps us from Jesus. Sin is real and it will trip us up if not dealt with. Jesus dealt with sin on the cross. We deal with sin by casting it off at the cross.

Third, we have to keep Jesus in our view at all times. He has already run his race and he shows us how to run our race.

Fourth, we have to run the race with others. When it comes to following Jesus, lone runners don't fare well. Pack runners stay in the race for the long haul.

Have you forgotten the definition of your race? That the race is about following Jesus by faith? Is there sin you need to deal with? Are you keeping Jesus in view? Are you running the race with others? As you walk through your day, think about these points.

For consider him who endured such hostility from sinners against himself, so that you won't grow weary and give up. In struggling against sin, you have not yet resisted to the point of shedding your blood. And you have forgotten the exhortation that addresses you as sons: My son, do not take the Lord's discipline lightly or lose heart when you are reproved by him, for the Lord disciplines the one he loves and punishes every son he receives.

Endure suffering as discipline: God is dealing with you as sons. For what son is there that a father does not discipline? But if you are without discipline—which all receive—then you are illegitimate children and not sons. Furthermore, we had human fathers discipline us, and we respected them. Shouldn't we submit even more to the Father of spirits and live? For they disciplined us for a short time based on what seemed good to them, but he does it for our benefit, so that we can share his holiness. No discipline seems enjoyable at the time, but painful. Later on, however, it yields the peaceful fruit of righteousness to those who have been trained by it.

Therefore, strengthen your tired hands and weakened knees, and make straight paths for your feet, so that what is lame may not be dislocated but healed instead.

# Faint-Hearted or Faith-Hearted?

The experience of faith-testing struggles can cause faint-heartedness, or can be faced with faith-heartedness. Hebrews 12 shows us the way of faith.

Jesus endured hostility from sinful people in this world. That hostility eventually led to his crucifixion. But his suffering was meaningful. He proved himself completely obedient to God the Father, and he accomplished our salvation by dying for our sins.

By faith in Jesus Christ, our struggles and sufferings are transformed from meaningless occurrences to the means of God's work in our lives. Jesus sets us in the grace and care of God who is our Father. As our Father, God uses the struggles and sufferings of life to accomplish good, just as he did with Jesus. Faith-heartedness comes when we know our Father's love for us and his ways in our lives.

Here is a bold promise given to us by God through the apostle Paul in Romans 8:28: "All things work together for the good of those who love God, who are called according to his purpose." How can God make that promise? Because God is in control of all things, he cares for us, and he is active in our lives. Even when things are difficult or challenging, when we are met with the temptation to be faint-hearted, we can know that God is working our circumstances together for good. We will not understand this fully in this life, but the faith-hearted person takes hope in this promise.

Pray today that God would give you the ability to be faith-hearted, knowing that everything you face is meant for your good.

In addition, my brothers and sisters, rejoice in the Lord. To write to you again about this is no trouble for me and is a safeguard for you.

Watch out for the dogs, watch out for the evil workers, watch out for those who mutilate the flesh. For we are the circumcision, the ones who worship by the Spirit of God, boast in Christ Jesus, and do not put confidence in the flesh—although I have reasons for confidence in the flesh. If anyone else thinks he has grounds for confidence in the flesh, I have more: circumcised the eighth day; of the nation of Israel, of the tribe of Benjamin, a Hebrew born of Hebrews; regarding the law, a Pharisee; regarding zeal, persecuting the church; regarding the righteousness that is in the law, blameless.

But everything that was a gain to me, I have considered to be a loss because of Christ. More than that, I also consider everything to be a loss in view of the surpassing value of knowing Christ Jesus my Lord. Because of him I have suffered the loss of all things and consider them as dung, so that I may gain Christ and be found in him, not having a righteousness of my own from the law, but one that is through faith in Christ—the righteousness from God based on faith. My goal is to know him and the power of his resurrection and the fellowship of his sufferings, being conformed to his death, assuming that I will somehow reach the resurrection from among the dead.

# Rejoice

Joy is more than a feeling. It is a necessity. "The joy of the LORD is your strength" (Neh. 8:10). We need strength of mind, emotion, and resolve. We need strengthened hope for today and tomorrow. We need strengthened confidence that our past will not come back to condemn us. We need strength to travel on the road of discipleship with Jesus and seek first his kingdom. Joy in the Lord provides this strength.

Philippians 3 begins with the command to "rejoice in the Lord." To rejoice is to take joy in something and to express that joy. In this chapter, we see what the Lord has provided for our rejoicing. The first eleven verses in particular show us two great causes of rejoicing for the Christian.

1. Rejoice that God calls out a people from the world to be his worshipers, and that he provides the way for his people to worship him (vv. 1–6).

Humans were made to know the joy of worshiping God. Human rebellion against God has shut down that worship, but God, in mercy, has made the way for us to return to it, and to know the joy of the Lord. That way is by the new birth of the Spirit and the sin-removing cross of Jesus Christ. When we repent of our rebellion and trust wholly in Jesus, we are made right with God. This is a great joy.

2. Rejoice that God grants us right standing with himself and a relationship with his Son, Jesus Christ (vv. 7–11).

Just as we were made for the worship of God, we were also made for relationship with his Son, Jesus Christ. Joy comes from the worship of God in all his grandeur and a relationship with the Son in the shared experience of his suffering, death, and resurrection power.

To relate to the Son, we must be made righteous in the Son. We must possess the righteousness of Jesus Christ by virtue of it being granted to us by faith. Only then can we know the Son in the intimacy of relationship and personal experience. To know the Son is to have joy.

As you meditate on these reasons for rejoicing, I pray that you will be strengthened for a life of following Christ today.

## ——— Romans 5:6–11 ———

For while we were still helpless, at the right time, Christ died for the ungodly. For rarely will someone die for a just person—though for a good person perhaps someone might even dare to die. But God proves his own love for us in that while we were still sinners, Christ died for us. How much more then, since we have now been declared righteous by his blood, will we be saved through him from wrath. For if, while we were enemies, we were reconciled to God through the death of his Son, then how much more, having been reconciled, will we be saved by his life. And not only that, but we also rejoice in God through our Lord Jesus Christ, through whom we have now received this reconciliation.

# Joy in God

The summit of the gospel mountain is God. Jesus is the road that gets us to God so that we would enjoy him. That is the central message of Romans 5:6–11.

The first chapters of Romans are a lengthy discussion of sin, wrath, the death of Christ for our sins, grace, faith, justification, and reconciliation with God. Reading these chapters is like starting at the base of a mountain and trekking to the top. At the top is joy in God.

Romans 5:11 tells us that by faith in Jesus Christ we are reconciled to God. Jesus died on the cross to pay the penalty for our sins. When we repent of our sins and believe in Christ, we are brought into friendship with God. As God's friends, we have joy in him. Joy in God is the summit experience of the gospel.

I pray today that you would have joy in God. The book of Romans reveals that the ultimate human experience is joy in God, and that joy in him produces much fruit.

- The fruit of God's glory—May we enjoy God so much that he is seen as valuable, beautiful, and worthy of our highest allegiance.
- The fruit of endurance—May the weary and distracted endure in faith and obedience because of the joy that is certainly ours both now and in eternity.
- The fruit of purity—May the desire for joy in God cause us to kill every sin that threatens to interfere. May we fight temptation with the promise of great joy in a life of purity.
- The fruit of love—May we be known as the people who know how to love, because the love of God is poured out within our hearts, creating a joy that overflows for others.
- The fruit of evangelism—May our joy in God be contagious. May we find ourselves inviting others to enter the joy of God through repentance and faith in Christ.
- The fruit of worship—When we gather with our churches, when we rise early in the morning, as we fall asleep at night, as we do our daily tasks, may we lift our souls to God in exultation.

"Now to him who is able to protect you from stumbling and to make you stand in the presence of his glory, without blemish and with great joy, to the only God our Savior, through Jesus Christ our Lord, be glory, majesty, power, and authority before all time, now and forever. Amen" (Jude 24–25).

## PHILIPPIANS 1:3–5

I give thanks to my God for every remembrance of you, always praying with joy for all of you in my every prayer, because of your partnership in the gospel from the first day until now.

# Finding Joy

Some of what you experience today, this week, and this year, will bring you joy—some will not. Joy seems so uncertain because our experiences are so unpredictable.

Is there a sure way to find joy? Is there a stable place to attach our joy?

Philippians 1 has a great deal to say about finding joy in the good news of Jesus Christ. With the apostle Paul as our guide and the Philippian church as our example, we see in this letter how joy comes from growing in the grace of the gospel, participating in the advance of the gospel, and sharing together in a life that reflects the gospel.

Consider reading the entire chapter today, and as you do, consider the following.

1. Think about all the places you are seeking to find joy and all the ways you are trying to secure it. Ask yourself these questions: Am I seeking joy in things that will produce it in lasting measure? Is my search for joy based on a foundation that can bear up under the weight of my expectations?

2. Look for the ways joy comes to Paul and to these Christians. Are there ways you need to shift your thinking about joy and how to find it?

3. Pray. Ask the Lord to prepare you for all that you will face today. Ask for the power of God's Spirit to work in you.

4. Go. By faith, step into your day seeking joy in Christ and an opportunity to show love to others.

## 1 CORINTHIANS 5:9–13

I wrote to you in a letter not to associate with sexually immoral people. I did not mean the immoral people of this world or the greedy and swindlers or idolaters; otherwise you would have to leave the world. But
actually, I wrote you not to associate with anyone who
claims to be a brother or sister and is sexually immoral
or greedy, an idolater or verbally abusive, a drunkard
or a swindler. Do not even eat with such a person. For
what business is it of mine to judge outsiders? Don't
you judge those who are inside? God judges outsiders.
Remove the evil person from among you.

# In the World

Bob Briner, author of *Roaring Lambs,* used to say, "God's power to preserve is greater than Satan's power to corrupt."[7]

Bob would say this when he talked about how reluctant and afraid Christians often are to associate with the world. Bob knew what he was talking about. He was a sports journalist, television producer, and agent for athletes. He certainly mixed it up with the world. He knew God's faithfulness to keep him faithful to Christ in his associations with people in what we would call "worldly" settings.

Before he passed away several years ago, Bob gave the church I pastor a vision for engagement in the world. He taught us that not everyone is called to be a pastor or missionary, but that all Christians are called to be salt and light in the world. He told us all Christians can mix it up with unbelievers and in worldly places for the sake of the gospel. He called us to be wise and careful, but not fearful, in engaging the world. He reminded us of the promises and power of God that keep us faithful to Christ.

In 1 Corinthians 5, Paul tells the church not to associate with a professing believer who had given himself to the sexually immoral lifestyle that Jesus died to save him from. Paul found it necessary to clarify, however, that he did not want believers in the church to disassociate from unbelievers in the world, for then they would have to go out of the world. The implication is that, rather than go out of the world, which we cannot do, we should live and engage purposefully in the world for the glory of God.

I hope this truth will further shape and sharpen your vision for the kind of engagement with the world that will bring the gospel to people and glory to Christ. Christ's vision for his church isn't one of disengagement, but of purposeful engagement with a world that desperately needs him.

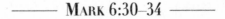

## Mark 6:30–34

The apostles gathered around Jesus and reported to him all that they had done and taught. He said to them, "Come away by yourselves to a remote place and rest for a while." For many people were coming and going, and they did not even have time to eat.

So they went away in the boat by themselves to a remote place, but many saw them leaving and recognized them, and they ran on foot from all the towns and arrived ahead of them.

When he went ashore, he saw a large crowd and had compassion on them, because they were like sheep without a shepherd. Then he began to teach them many things.

# Seeing People with New Eyes

What do you see when you look at people?

Do you see differences that make you angry or uncomfortable? Demands that make you want to turn and walk the other way? Obstacles to your agenda for the day? A personal threat? Maybe you see the means to your own end. Oh, how we need new eyes.

One day Jesus was tired and needed rest. He didn't have enough time to eat because so many people were asking for his attention. When he went away with his disciples, the crowd of people followed him, caught up with him, and asked for more. Jesus had every reason to be exasperated and to see in this crowd more demands, problems, expectations, and inconveniences than he could handle.

Instead, he "had compassion on them, because they were like sheep without a shepherd" (Mark 6:34).

Jesus saw the people who were standing in front of him with eyes focused by purpose, love, and compassion. His purpose was to glorify God and shepherd the people by dying for their sins and rising for their life. He loved them because they were humans created in God's image. He had compassion on them because they were in need.

We are these people. We know God, are forgiven of our sins, and have eternal life because Jesus looked on us with compassion and called us to repentance and faith.

Jesus is our Shepherd. We follow him. Now we need his eyes to see people as he did.

Seeing people with new eyes is a requirement for carrying out the Great Commission to preach the gospel to the world. The desire for God's glory and genuine love for others sharpens our focus to see like Jesus did. Compassion changes how we look at people. Pray today that God would give you the compassion that he has for people, that you may be compelled to carry out the Great Commission he has given us.

—— 1 Corinthians 10:31 ——

So, whether you eat or drink, or whatever you do,
do everything for the glory of God.

# A New Way to Walk in the World

We need wisdom to walk this way. There are many issues and opportunities in life that require us to think about the best way to glorify God. At times the questions of life have a simple, straightforward answer. Don't steal, murder, or commit adultery. Do honor your parents, love your neighbor, and tell the truth. At other times, things are not quite so clear. But that doesn't mean we have no guidance for a way forward that brings glory to God.

First Corinthians 8, 9, and 10 give us wisdom. I encourage you today, or this week, to read all three of these chapters.

From 1 Corinthians 8, consider what builds up the faith of other Christians. Thinking about how to serve the spiritual growth of your fellow church members can help you make good decisions about how to live in the world.

From 1 Corinthians 9, consider what commends the gospel to people in the world. Making decisions about your interactions in the world based on how people need to hear the gospel is a great way to glorify God.

From 1 Corinthians 10, consider what promotes devotion to Christ in your own life. Every day we make big and small decisions that can either harm or enhance our obedience to God.

This is a big chunk of the Bible, written by the apostle Paul almost two thousand years ago. This wisdom still applies to us. My prayer is that as you think on these things, the Lord will give you understanding for how to glorify him as you walk in the world.

Although I am free from all and not anyone's slave, I have made myself a slave to everyone, in order to win more people. To the Jews I became like a Jew, to win Jews; to those under the law, like one under the law — though I myself am not under the law — to win those under the law. To those who are without the law, like one without the law — though I am not without God's law but under the law of Christ — to win those without the law. To the weak I became weak, in order to win the weak. I have become all things to all people, so that I may by every possible means save some. Now I do all this because of the gospel, so that I may share in the blessings.

# World Christians

What did Paul mean when he said that he "have become all things to all people . . . because of the gospel" (vv. 22–23)? This is what D. A. Carson calls becoming a world Christian. Carson describes a world Christian as someone for whom the following things are true:

> Their allegiance to Jesus Christ and his kingdom is above all national, cultural, linguistic, and racial allegiances. Their commitment to the church is to the church everywhere and not only to the church on home turf. They see themselves first and foremost as citizens of the heavenly kingdom. As a result, they are single-minded and sacrificial when it comes to the paramount mandate to evangelize and make disciples.[8]

World Christians are concerned with the spread of the gospel and the growth of the church around the world. And, you can be a world Christian without leaving your hometown. But if being a world Christian involves crossing national, cultural, linguistic, and racial boundaries, how can someone be a world Christian without leaving home?

1. Find out how many people groups live in your area. Chances are, there are not only several different people groups, but maybe even some unreached people groups near you. For the purposes of evangelism and church planting, we call a people group "unreached" when it has no witness of the gospel or church in its own language and culture. In Nashville, where I live and pastor, there are approximately thirty unreached people groups.

2. Identify another country or people group in a part of the world, and pray specifically for that area. Pray for the church there, that the Spirit would empower and encourage and build her. Pray that unbelievers there would repent and believe in Jesus.

3. Be a part of a church that supports and sends people around the world. If your church is a sending church in this way, support that by giving time, money, and prayer. If not, encourage your church to begin considering how it can be obedient to the Great Commission by sending and supporting people around the world who go to other nations and people groups.

You can become all things to all people where you live by crossing cultural divides and shaping your life accordingly. By doing so, you can help the gospel be heard among the various people groups of the world.

An angel of the Lord spoke to Philip: "Get up and go south to the road that goes down from Jerusalem to Gaza." (This is the desert road.) So he got up and went. There was an Ethiopian man, a eunuch and high official of Candace, queen of the Ethiopians, who was in charge of her entire treasury. He had come to worship in Jerusalem and was sitting in his chariot on his way home, reading the prophet Isaiah aloud.

The Spirit told Philip, "Go and join that chariot."

When Philip ran up to it, he heard him reading the prophet Isaiah, and said, "Do you understand what you're reading?"

"How can I," he said, "unless someone guides me?" So he invited Philip to come up and sit with him. Now the Scripture passage he was reading was this:

"He was led like a sheep to the slaughter, and as a lamb is silent before its shearer, so he does not open his mouth. In his humiliation justice was denied him.

"Who will describe his generation? For his life is taken from the earth."

The eunuch said to Philip, "I ask you, who is the prophet saying this about—himself or someone else?"

Philip proceeded to tell him the good news about Jesus, beginning with that Scripture.

As they were traveling down the road, they came to some water. The eunuch said, "Look, there's water. What would keep me from being baptized?" So he ordered the chariot to stop, and both Philip and the eunuch went down into the water, and he baptized him. When they came up out of the water, the Spirit of the Lord carried Philip away, and the eunuch did not see him any longer but went on his way rejoicing.

# Engage One

If I were in charge of getting the message of Jesus to all the nations on earth, I would probably not return your call or answer your email.

The calls I would make would be to the Christian leaders around the world. I would gather them together and the biggest brainstorm session known to man would commence. We would establish an evangelism and church planting philosophy, define the mission, set goals, hammer out a strategy, and secure the necessary funding for the task.

You, I'm sure, would understand if I simply couldn't get back to you.

Thankfully, I am not in charge of world evangelization. And no one has to wait until a committee figures out how to do it until he or she shares the gospel or has a chance to hear it.

In Acts 8 we see that God is in charge of his mission and that he accomplishes it in unexpected ways. First, God used persecution due to preaching about Jesus in Jerusalem to spread the gospel beyond the city and into the surrounding region. The Christians who were scattered by the persecution simply sowed the gospel seed as they went. The persecution wasn't good, but God used it for good as his Spirit-filled church remained faithful to the mission.

Then there is the account of one man (Philip) who engaged with another man (an Ethiopian) for a one-on-one conversation about the Bible and Jesus (while in a chariot on a hot desert road). The spread of the gospel to all the nations includes individual encounters. Names are given.

The account of Philip and the Ethiopian has lessons for us on numerous levels. One is that God has his ways, and by his Spirit he leads one person to engage in a conversation about Jesus with another person. This is how God advances his mission in the world. There is a place for the task force, and God uses big events in history for good, but one thing that should not be missed in the mission of God is the way the gospel moves forward one conversation at a time.

Consider today if there is anyone with whom you need to have a one-on-one conversation with about Jesus. Pray for the courage to obey, and to take part in God's strategy for accomplishing his mission.

When the day of Pentecost had arrived, they were all together in one place. Suddenly a sound like that of a violent rushing wind came from heaven, and it filled the whole house where they were staying. They saw tongues like flames of fire that separated and rested on each one of them. Then they were all filled with the Holy Spirit and began to speak in different tongues, as the Spirit enabled them.

Now there were Jews staying in Jerusalem, devout people from every nation under heaven. When this sound occurred, a crowd came together and was confused because each one heard them speaking in his own language. They were astounded and amazed, saying, "Look, aren't all these who are speaking Galileans? How is it that each of us can hear them in our own native language? Parthians, Medes, Elamites; those who live in Mesopotamia, in Judea and Cappadocia, Pontus and Asia, Phrygia and Pamphylia, Egypt and the parts of Libya near Cyrene; visitors from Rome (both Jews and converts), Cretans and Arabs—we hear them declaring the magnificent acts of God in our own tongues." They were all astounded and perplexed, saying to one another, "What does this mean?" But some sneered and said, "They're drunk on new wine."

# Messaging

There are times when people repeat back to me what they think I said in a sermon or a conversation. I am often surprised that what they heard is not what I meant to say. I have learned the importance of staying on message and speaking as clearly as possible.

The problem is not always how I speak, but how others hear. I may say what I mean to say, and say it clearly, but people hear some other message for their own reasons. I have also learned the importance of asking people what they are hearing me say.

Messaging is important. Two key questions we should always ask are, "What am I saying?" and "What are others hearing?"

In Acts 2, we see that the Holy Spirit is very interested in messaging. The Holy Spirit filled the disciples of Jesus with his power, loosed their tongues to speak in the languages of the multi-national crowd around them, and led them to tell of the mighty works of God. The Holy Spirit worked in the minds and mouths of the disciples to keep God's power and grace their main message, and to speak it clearly.

The Holy Spirit was also active in the people who gathered around the disciples to ensure that they heard the message being spoken. The gift of speaking in tongues given to the disciples was the ability to speak in the languages of the people listening. The purpose of this gift was so that many would hear of the mighty works of God.

Where the Holy Spirit is active, good messaging takes place. Spirit-filled people tell of the works of God. Spirit-drawn people hear the message and are stirred to ask, "What does this mean?" Telling and hearing of the mighty works of God opens the door for the gospel of Jesus Christ.

We all experience communication breakdowns. We know the challenges of good messaging. But the master communicator, who keeps the message clear and ensures that it is heard, is the Holy Spirit.

We are not called to passively sit back and wait for God's Spirit to fill the church and lead people to faith. We are called to pray. To ask God to work through his message and to ensure that it is heard and responded to through our obedience in telling it. Today, will you pray for Spirit-filled messaging among your church and the churches in your city and around the world?

## 2 Corinthians 4:1–15

Therefore, since we have this ministry because we were shown mercy, we do not give up. Instead, we have renounced secret and shameful things, not acting deceitfully or distorting the word of God, but commending ourselves before God to everyone's conscience by an open display of the truth. But if our gospel is veiled, it is veiled to those who are perishing. In their case, the god of this age has blinded the minds of the unbelievers to keep them from seeing the light of the gospel of the glory of Christ, who is the image of God. For we are not proclaiming ourselves but Jesus Christ as Lord, and ourselves as your servants for Jesus' sake. For God who said, "Let light shine out of darkness," has shone in our hearts to give the light of the knowledge of God's glory in the face of Jesus Christ.

Now we have this treasure in clay jars, so that this extraordinary power may be from God and not from us. We are afflicted in every way but not crushed; we are perplexed but not in despair; we are persecuted but not abandoned; we are struck down but not destroyed. We always carry the death of Jesus in our body, so that the life of Jesus may also be displayed in our body. For we who live are always being given over to death for Jesus's sake, so that Jesus's life may also be displayed in our mortal flesh. So then, death is at work in us, but life in you. And since we have the same spirit of faith in keeping with what is written, "I believed, therefore I spoke," we also believe, and therefore speak. For we know that the one who raised the Lord Jesus will also raise us with Jesus and present us with you. Indeed, everything is for your benefit so that, as grace extends through more and more people, it may cause thanksgiving to increase to the glory of God.

# Treasure in Clay Jars

In 2 Corinthians 4:7, the apostle Paul said, "we have this treasure in clay jars." The jar of clay is a metaphor for the weakness and ordinariness of our humanity. Don't miss this. Paul is saying that God has entrusted the gospel of the glory of Christ to weak and ordinary people.

Oh, how we avoid our weakness! To do so, we even change the meaning of the metaphor. We say jars of clay are works of art, quaint, cute, and collector's items. But really, they were necessities of the day. They were everywhere (ordinary) and they broke easily (weak). Don't make the mistake of changing the meaning of the metaphor to avoid weakness. Receive the metaphor as a statement of your humanity and the weakness and ordinariness that comes with it. It is in jars of clay (ordinary, weak humans) that God has entrusted the gospel. The reason he has done so is to show his power.

Here is the mystery of God's power. He shows it in human weakness. Did not his own Son, Jesus, become a weak and humble man to show the power of God to save us from our sins (Phil. 2:7–8)?

Your confidence is not in yourself, but in God who shows his power in your weakness. Today, as you sense your weakness, yield yourself to God. Ask for the power of his Spirit to live in and through you. Then, get on with what he has called you to do. Your weakness is not a disqualifier for doing the will of God. It is the place that God demonstrates his power so you can do his will, for his glory and your joy.

For the word of the cross is foolishness to those who are perishing, but it is the power of God to us who are being saved.

For it is written, I will destroy the wisdom of the wise, and I will set aside the intelligence of the intelligent.

Where is the one who is wise? Where is the teacher of the law? Where is the debater of this age? Hasn't God made the world's wisdom foolish? For since, in God's wisdom, the world did not know God through wisdom, God was pleased to save those who believe through the foolishness of what is preached. For the Jews ask for signs and the Greeks seek wisdom, but we preach Christ crucified, a stumbling block to the Jews and foolishness to the Gentiles. Yet to those who are called, both Jews and Greeks, Christ is the power of God and the wisdom of God, because God's foolishness is wiser than human wisdom, and God's weakness is stronger than human strength.

Brothers and sisters, consider your calling: Not many were wise from a human perspective, not many powerful, not many of noble birth. Instead, God has chosen what is foolish in the world to shame the wise, and God has chosen what is weak in the world to shame the strong. God has chosen what is insignificant and despised in the world—what is viewed as nothing—to bring to nothing what is viewed as something, so that no one may boast in his presence. It is from him that you are in Christ Jesus, who became wisdom from God for us—our righteousness, sanctification, and redemption, in order that, as it is written: Let the one who boasts, boast in the Lord.

# Shaped by the Cross or the Culture?

Whenever Christians talk about the culture, the conversation can go in one of two directions. We can talk about how bad the culture is and how we should stay as far away from it as possible (which is impossible), or we can talk about how much we need to be like the culture in order to be relevant in our representation of Christianity and presentation of the gospel (which is unwise).

In 1 Corinthians, we hear the apostle Paul calling the church to be shaped by the message of the cross of Christ and not by the culture's message of power and wisdom. There is no mention of cultural disengagement or isolation; yet neither is there a call to be like the culture to appear relevant. Rather, here is a clear call to embrace the power and wisdom of God in the cross of Christ. By doing so, we will have a true and saving message for the culture in which we live.

It is important to ask ourselves, as Christians and congregations, *What have we been given and what are we to give that is unique to the Christian faith?* The answer, according to this passage, is the message of the cross of Jesus Christ. In the cross of Christ is both the power to save people from the condemnation awaiting them due to their sin, and the knowledge of God that comes from being reconciled to him.

If, on the one hand, we are trying to separate ourselves from the "culture"—by which we usually mean people—then we will be ineffective in bringing the message of the cross to them. There will not be enough contact with people to have meaningful communication. And what little communication there is will not be accompanied by love, empathy, and humility.

On the other hand, if our priority is to be like the culture—by which we usually mean liked by people—then we will be tempted to downplay the message of the cross if it initially seems foolish to others. Then, as people come to the end of themselves because of the emptiness of their sin and turn to the church for some word of hope, we will not have one. We will have lost it in the name of "relevance." We will have become irrelevant to their real need.

Pray today that you will keep the word of the cross strong in your heart, constant in your congregational relationships, and always with you as you live fully engaged in the world.

## Romans 12:14–16

Bless those who persecute you; bless and do not curse. Rejoice with those who rejoice; weep with those who weep. Live in harmony with one another. Do not be proud; instead, associate with the humble. Do not be wise in your own estimation.

# A New Heart for Love

The most basic command in the Bible is to love. And yet, the most basic human failure is to not love well. For example, Romans 12:9 tells us to love genuinely. The following verses give us twenty-five commands that express love. We have violated every one of these commands by either omission or commission. What a pitiful record of love we have. What are we going to do? Where will we find the love we are commanded to express to others?

The answer is in the gospel. This is how the prophet Ezekiel described the gospel: "I will give you a new heart and put a new spirit within you; I will remove your heart of stone and give you a heart of flesh. I will place my Spirit within you and cause you to follow my statutes and carefully observe my ordinances" (Ezek. 36:26–27). The gospel is the message that God makes our hearts new, so that from the heart we will obey his command to love.

Here's the way this same gospel message is put by the apostle Paul. "Now the goal of our instruction [the gospel] is love that comes from a pure heart, a good conscience, and a sincere faith" (1 Tim. 1:5). Again we are told that love comes from a new heart.

If we are to love as Christ loves us and as he has commanded us to love others, we must have hearts made new in three ways.

First, to love, we must have a sincere faith. Our faith must be in Jesus Christ alone for salvation. Our sins are forgiven and we are made right with God by faith in Christ. When we trust Christ in this way, he makes us new people. He changes our hearts. Love flows from this new heart.

Second, to love, we must have a good conscience. Christ cleanses our conscience when he forgives our sins. Through active faith in Christ and obedience to him, we maintain a clear conscience before others. The clean heart is free to love.

Third, to love we must have a pure heart. Purity means a single focus on one love. This one love is Christ. When the heart is pure toward Christ, it takes on the character of Christ, which is love for others.

If we want to love well, we must tend to our hearts. Faith, forgiveness, and focus on Christ alone fill our hearts with love and produce a fountain of love for others.

## HEBREWS 13:1–6

Let brotherly love continue. Don't neglect to show hospitality, for by doing this some have welcomed angels as guests without knowing it. Remember those in prison, as though you were in prison with them, and the mistreated, as though you yourselves were suffering bodily. Marriage is to be honored by all and the marriage bed kept undefiled, because God will judge the sexually immoral and adulterers. Keep your life free from the love of money. Be satisfied with what you have, for he himself has said, I will never leave you or abandon you. Therefore, we may boldly say, The Lord is my helper; I will not be afraid. What can man do to me?

# Let Brotherly Love Continue

Hebrews 13:1–6 tells Christians to let love endure. We are to let love continue to come from our lives in very practical ways. The expressions of love in this passage are hospitality, empathy, fidelity in marriage, and contentment with what we have, rather than a dominating love of money.

Underneath these commands are questions for the heart. Why don't we express love? What is going on in our hearts when we don't let love continue? What do we have from God that changes our hearts so we can endure in love for others?

Fundamentally, failure to love is due to a preoccupation with self. Self-lordship leaves little room for love. Why the preoccupation with self? One reason is that we mistakenly believe that no one, not even God, will care and provide for us. So, we must.

Sometimes we are left to care for ourselves without the aid of others. But the Christian is never left without the care and provision of God.

At the end of this passage, we hear two promises from God that have the power to dethrone self. One is the promise of God's presence. He says, "I will never leave you or abandon you." The other is the promise of God's help. "The Lord is my helper; I will not be afraid."

The presence and help of the Lord free us from the false notion that we are alone and that we must take care of ourselves. Taking these promises to heart helps free us from being preoccupied with self so we can love others well.

Today, turn your eyes to Jesus. Focus on the God who promises to never leave you or abandon you, the God who is your helper. Pray that as you look to him, he would cause you to abandon your focus on self, so that you can love him and love others well.

## 1 CORINTHIANS 13:1–13

If I speak human or angelic tongues but do not have love, I am a noisy gong or a clanging cymbal. If I have the gift of prophecy and understand all mysteries and all knowledge, and if I have all faith so that I can move mountains but do not have love, I am nothing. And if I give away all my possessions, and if I give over my body in order to boast but do not have love, I gain nothing.

Love is patient, love is kind. Love does not envy, is not boastful, is not arrogant, is not rude, is not self-seeking, is not irritable, and does not keep a record of wrongs. Love finds no joy in unrighteousness but rejoices in the truth. It bears all things, believes all things, hopes all things, endures all things.

Love never ends. But as for prophecies, they will come to an end; as for tongues, they will cease; as for knowledge, it will come to an end. For we know in part, and we prophesy in part, but when the perfect comes, the partial will come to an end. When I was a child, I spoke like a child, I thought like a child, I reasoned like a child. When I became a man, I put aside childish things. For now we see only a reflection as in a mirror, but then face to face. Now I know in part, but then I will know fully, as I am fully known. Now these three remain: faith, hope, and love—but the greatest of these is love.

# Loving the Church

Whenever I hear people say they love their church, I wonder if what they really mean is that they love something *about* their church. I assume that they like something about the style of music, the preaching, the building, or the demographic makeup of their church. I wonder, if that something were no longer a part of their church, would they still love it?

Why should we love the church? We are human, so it is natural to prefer one church to others based on tangibles like preaching, music, and friends. But should these things be the basis of our love for the church, and for the particular church to which we belong?

The book of Ephesians gives us three good reasons to love the church.

1. Christ died for the church (Eph. 5:25). As followers of Jesus, how could we not deeply love and cherish what he gave his life to redeem?
2. In Christ, we belong to the church (Eph. 2:16). Though there are problems to work through in every church, and though it is sometimes necessary to move from one church to another, we cannot stop belonging to the church any more than we can stop belonging to Christ.
3. God is glorified in Christ and in the church (Eph. 3:21). There is simply no greater way that God has designed to display his greatness and grace on this earth than in his Son Jesus Christ and in the church he redeemed. God chose the church, loves the church, and displays his glory in the world through the church.

Consider the love that Paul defines in 1 Corinthians 13. Do you have this kind of love for your church? If not, pray that God would help you to love the church body to which you belong.

## 1 CORINTHIANS 12:1–11

Now concerning spiritual gifts: brothers and sisters, I do not want you to be unaware. You know that when you were pagans, you used to be enticed and led astray by mute idols. Therefore I want you to know that no one speaking by the Spirit of God says, "Jesus is cursed," and no one can say, "Jesus is Lord," except by the Holy Spirit.

Now there are different gifts, but the same Spirit. There are different ministries, but the same Lord. And there are different activities, but the same God produces each gift in each person. A manifestation of the Spirit is given to each person for the common good: to one is given a message of wisdom through the Spirit, to another, a message of knowledge by the same Spirit, to another, faith by the same Spirit, to another, gifts of healing by the one Spirit, to another, the performing of miracles, to another, prophecy, to another, distinguishing between spirits, to another, different kinds of tongues, to another, interpretation of tongues. One and the same Spirit is active in all these, distributing to each person as he wills.

# Spiritual Matters

Christians have forever asked what it means to be spiritual. What spiritual experiences must we have, what knowledge must we attain, and what personality must we possess to be spiritual? That is the question Paul addresses in 1 Corinthians 12.

The world of the Corinthian Christians included a variety of spiritual experiences. Before they came to faith in Christ, many of them were regularly at the pagan temples offering prayers and sacrifices and participating in physical and emotional expressions of worship. Now they are Christians. So how should they think about spiritual matters? What matters spiritually?

Paul teaches these Christians that spirituality comes from the Holy Spirit. The Holy Spirit leads a person from loyalty to personal and cultural idols to the confession that Jesus is Lord through repentance and faith. That same person is then given gifts and empowered to serve the common good of the church. The church where believers are confessing the lordship of Christ and being strengthened by service to one another then communicates the power of the gospel to the world.

What is your vision of spirituality? This vision of spirituality in 1 Corinthians is centered on God, grows from the gospel, builds the church, and witnesses to the world. Remember, anything that misses the mark on one of those four things is not from the Spirit of God.

## 2 CORINTHIANS 1:3–11

Blessed be the God and Father of our Lord Jesus Christ, the Father of mercies and the God of all comfort. He comforts us in all our affliction, so that we may be able to comfort those who are in any kind of affliction, through the comfort we ourselves receive from God. For just as the sufferings of Christ overflow to us, so also through Christ our comfort overflows. If we are afflicted, it is for your comfort and salvation. If we are comforted, it is for your comfort, which produces in you patient endurance of the same sufferings that we suffer. And our hope for you is firm, because we know that as you share in the sufferings, so you will also share in the comfort.

We don't want you to be unaware, brothers and sisters, of our affliction that took place in Asia. We were completely overwhelmed—beyond our strength—so that we even despaired of life itself. Indeed, we felt that we had received the sentence of death, so that we would not trust in ourselves but in God who raises the dead. He has delivered us from such a terrible death, and he will deliver us. We have put our hope in him that he will deliver us again while you join in helping us by your prayers. Then many will give thanks on our behalf for the gift that came to us through the prayers of many.

# Comfort One Another

There is a small group of pastors with whom I often gather for conversation. We do this regularly enough to have developed a pattern. We each take our turn giving a brief update on life and ministry. Then we put our leadership challenges on the table for all to speak into.

In one meeting we didn't get through the update round before one pastor laid his soul bare. He was struggling. At that point I watched with joy as the others of us brought comfort and encouragement to him. I noticed that the comfort given was from the heart of men who had themselves struggled and been comforted by God in various ways. We weren't spouting off like Job's friends; we were sharing the grace we had received.

This kind of mutual ministry is what we read about in 2 Corinthians. This letter is autobiographical. The apostle Paul opens up his life and heart to the church in Corinth. He asks the church to open up their hearts to him. Their mutual ministry was to bring the comfort of Christ in each other's afflictions and the strength of Christ to each one's weakness.

Have you ever been a part of the mutual ministry of comfort and strength in Christ? This ministry is one of the rich experiences of being connected to Christ and his people. In this ministry, we simply give the grace we have received. Paul calls it, "comforting others with the comfort with which we have been comforted" (2 Cor. 1:4, author's paraphrase).

I pray that you are in community in a place of genuine ministry that brings Christ to afflicted souls in a way that comforts and gives strength—a church that comforts with the comfort it has received.

Consider today where you can play a part in the comfort-giving ministry of God's people.

## PHILIPPIANS 4:1–3

So then, my dearly loved and longed for brothers and sisters, my joy and crown, in this manner stand firm in the Lord, dear friends.

I urge Euodia and I urge Syntyche to agree in the Lord. Yes, I also ask you, true partner, to help these women who have contended for the gospel at my side, along with Clement and the rest of my coworkers whose names are in the book of life.

# Agreement and Unity in the Church

Be honest. There are some people you prefer to be with more than others. And there are some people you prefer not to be with at all. There are some people you find agreeable. There are others with whom you disagree.

Now be really honest. You like some people more than others, and some people you don't like at all, *even in the church*. Sometimes you find yourself disagreeing with people you really love and that disagreement puts a strain on the relationship. That's a hard reality to deal with.

Here's another honesty check. You sometimes handle these situations and relationships with no thoughtful guiding principles, but simply by emotion. The relationship just happens, develops, or dissolves based on how you feel.

So what do you do when you read Bible passages about loving and living in unity with others in the church? How do you approach disagreement and disunity with your brothers and sisters in Christ?

The book of Philippians has much to say about Christian unity. This passage deals with a real disagreement between two members of the same church (Phil. 4:1–3). Here are a few highlights from this passage:

1. Christians need to keep in mind that we are in relationship with one another because we share the common experience of God's grace in Christ. We are united to one another as Christians, so the goal is to live like it. Focusing on the common experience of grace keeps us humble with each other.

2. Your agreement with other believers and church members doesn't have to be in everything (like food, music, politics, or even some local church practices). Rather, your agreement is in the gospel. Our unity of thought (Phil. 2:2) is about the events, meaning, response to, and experience of the incarnation, death, resurrection, ascension, and return of Jesus Christ. Our unity of practice is the love, holiness, worship, and ministry that flow from our faith.

3. Our agreement with one another and unity in the church is for the work of the Lord and the advance of the gospel. Agreement in the gospel and unity in relationships inspire and fuel partnerships for discipleship and congregational care, evangelism, and service in the world.

Think about the relationships you have that are strained, cool, or distant. Are you approaching or avoiding them based on emotion and convenience? Or are the grace, gospel, and work of the Lord providing you with reasons to live in love, unity, and agreement with your brothers and sisters in Christ? Think on these things.

## 1 Corinthians 11:2–16

Now I praise you because you remember me in everything and hold fast to the traditions just as I delivered them to you. But I want you to know that Christ is the head of every man, and the man is the head of the woman, and God is the head of Christ. Every man who prays or prophesies with something on his head dishonors his head. Every woman who prays or prophesies with her head uncovered dishonors her head, since that is one and the same as having her head shaved. For if a woman doesn't cover her head, she should have her hair cut off. But if it is disgraceful for a woman to have her hair cut off or her head shaved, let her head be covered.

A man should not cover his head, because he is the image and glory of God. So too, woman is the glory of man. For man did not come from woman, but woman came from man. Neither was man created for the sake of woman, but woman for the sake of man. This is why a woman should have a symbol of authority on her head, because of the angels. In the Lord, however, woman is not independent of man, and man is not independent of woman. For just as woman came from man, so man comes through woman, and all things come from God.

Judge for yourselves: Is it proper for a woman to pray to God with her head uncovered? Does not even nature itself teach you that if a man has long hair it is a disgrace to him, but that if a woman has long hair, it is her glory? For her hair is given to her as a covering. If anyone wants to argue about this, we have no other custom, nor do the churches of God.

# The Way We Come to Church Matters

The discussion in 1 Corinthians 11–14 is carried along by the phrase, "When you meet together." These four chapters are about what we call "going to church."

Paul addresses three different issues in the worship gatherings in Corinth: head coverings, the Lord's Supper, and the use of spiritual gifts. But the commonality in these issues was the way each person showed up to church. If they were focused on themselves, their worship was confusing and distracting. If they were focused on Christ, the edification of the church, and the clear communication of the gospel, their worship brought glory to God.

These chapters remind us that the way we come to church matters. That doesn't mean that we must be perfect in order to come to church. Nor does it mean we should stay away from church if we are struggling in our faith. In fact, attending church is exactly what we should do when we are struggling, for there we find Christ, his Word, and his people. It does mean that we can each prepare ourselves before we come to church.

Here are some questions you can pray through each weekend as you prepare for church on Sunday:

- Am I seeking God's glory as I worship and interact with people?
- Am I aware that God's grace in Christ is the reason I can enter into worship?
- Am I putting the focus on myself or on Christ in the way I worship and relate?
- Am I confusing or making clear the gospel of grace in the way I worship and relate?
- Are my relationships with others healthy?
- Is my attitude toward people who differ from me loving and accepting?
- Am I serving other people?

These questions are not meant to bind us up before we come to church, but rather to free us from ourselves, so that when we come to church, we worship God, build up one another, and communicate the gospel clearly.

## PHILIPPIANS 4:4–9

 Rejoice in the Lord always. I will say it again: Rejoice! Let your graciousness be known to everyone. The Lord is near. Don't worry about anything, but in everything, through prayer and petition with thanksgiving, present your requests to God. And the peace of God, which surpasses all understanding, will guard your hearts and minds in Christ Jesus.

 Finally brothers and sisters, whatever is true, whatever is honorable, whatever is just, whatever is pure, whatever is lovely, whatever is commendable—if there is any moral excellence and if there is anything praiseworthy—dwell on these things. Do what you have learned and received and heard from me, and seen in me, and the God of peace will be with you.

# When "You" Means "Y'all"

We read the Bible through the lens of individualism. I often preach that way. A discipline I am learning, is to read, think, pray, and live corporately.

Here's an example. Philippians 4 addresses prayer in anxiety; Paul encourages his audience to redirect their thinking to Christ. We read this passage as individuals. As we do, we are encouraged to think about our own lives. We apply this text to how we can practice prayer and discipline our minds to think well.

That's a good thing. We are disciples of Jesus Christ and each of us is called to follow him. But to limit our thinking only to the individual application of the Bible is not a good thing. In fact, it's not even the way the Bible was written.

In Philippians 4:8, the apostle Paul writes, "Finally brothers and sisters . . ." He is addressing a group we often refer to as "brethren," meaning the congregation. He is not addressing only the individuals in the congregation but the congregation as a whole. In the Southern United States, where I live, we distinguish between the individual "you" and the corporate "you." When there is more than one "you," it's "y'all." As we read through Philippians 4, it's helpful to hear Paul with a Southern accent.

Paul is addressing a church. He is applying the gospel to a congregation. As we interpret the passage, we should apply it to our congregations. As congregations spread all over the globe, we are here to be "lights in the world" (Phil. 2:15 ESV). By living in unity with one another, praying in our anxiety, and thinking on the things of Christ, a congregation does two things. First, it lives in contrast to the world (which is divided, reactionary, and thinks at a low level with no reference to Christ). Second, it shines as both a witness of the power of Christ and an invitation to come to him.

Read Philippians 4:4–9 again through a congregational lens. Consider how you can encourage your church to live as a corporate light in the world.

## —— Romans 12:10–13 ——

Let love be without hypocrisy. Detest evil; cling to what is good. Love one another deeply as brothers and sisters. Outdo one another in showing honor. Do not lack diligence in zeal; be fervent in the Spirit; serve the Lord. Rejoice in hope; be patient in affliction; be persistent in prayer. Share with the saints in their needs; pursue hospitality.

# Unmasked Love

You can't treat love like a mask used to cover up your true intentions. Genuine love is unmasked. The word *hypocrite* comes from the world of acting. The actor would wear a mask to portray his role, thus covering up his true identity. "Hypocrite" came to be used to refer to someone who in life was wearing a mask to cover up his true self.

Paul related the word *hypocrite* to love to communicate that we often pretend to be acting out of love to cover up the true motives behind our actions. He exhorted us to let our love be without hypocrisy, without a mask. Our love is to be real.

Real love doesn't mask a desire to use others to serve ourselves. This is not love but manipulation. When you serve others, let it be for their good, not so that you can later be paid back for your good.

Real love doesn't mask a need to build our reputation before others. When you serve others, don't worry about what they think of you. Don't be concerned about being seen by others. Just love.

Real love doesn't mask an attempt to achieve righteousness before God. Remember that there is no goodness you can do to attain a right relationship with God. That is his gift to you and you receive it by faith. In the freedom from the need to perform for righteousness, go love for the joy of it.

What should you do if you manipulate, are worried about your reputation, or find yourself trying to earn your righteousness before God? Repent and believe. Repent of self-service, of people pleasing, and of belittling the cross of Christ by believing you need your own goodness more than his. Turn to God in complete faith and trust. Ask him to show you the depth of his mercy toward you in Christ, and by it to generate in you sincere love for him and others.

### —— Romans 12:1–2 ——

Therefore, brothers and sisters, in view of the mercies of God, I urge you to present your bodies as a living sacrifice, holy and pleasing to God; this is your true worship. Do not be conformed to this age, but be transformed by the renewing of your mind, so that you may discern what is the good, pleasing, and perfect will of God.

# Moved by Mercy

After eleven chapters in Romans of pure mercy from God toward sinners, Paul opened chapter 12 of Romans with a strong exhortation. "I urge you," he said. In light of God's mercy in Christ, Paul wants to motivate the people to a new kind of living. In short, Christians are to be moved by mercy! How can you apply this to your life today?

1. Be moved by mercy by meditating on the mercy of God toward you in Christ. In *A Practical View of Christianity*, William Wilberforce includes a section on "Looking unto Jesus." He calls Christians to meditate on the cross of Christ as a way of ridding the heart of sin and building into our lives those qualities that please God. His point is that meditating on the mercy of the cross as our deliverance from sin and wrath moves us in practical, transforming ways. Many "secrets" and "discoveries" have been put forth as the way to live our faith with victory and joy. But there are no real secrets. The way has been laid out plainly for all to see. Meditate on the mercy of God in the cross of Christ.

2. Be moved toward God by mercy. Keep in view God's mercy for you in the past. He has cleansed you of every ugly sin you have committed in both deed and thought. Keep in view God's mercy for you in the present. You are breathing, working, living, and experiencing his grace this moment by his mercy. Keep in view God's mercy for you in the future. Your next hour will be supplied with what you need to love and obey God and to serve others by his mercy. Then, with this view of mercy, give yourself to God unreservedly and with great joy.

3. Be moved toward others by mercy. As one who has received mercy, go show mercy. Speak kindly to those who speak harshly. Give to those in need. Help the helpless. Bind up the broken and build up the beaten down. Fix something for someone. Support a child through a ministry. Encourage adoption. Discourage abortion. Resist racism. Feed the homeless. Visit an elderly person. Volunteer at a school. Baby-sit for parents. Use words to restore dignity to someone. Correct a friend who is sinning. Look for practical ways to be a mercy-giver in your home and workplace. In all things, take the opportunities you have to tell of the mercy of Christ in the cross that moves you to show and share mercy to others.

## ROMANS 12:1–2

Therefore, brothers and sisters, in view of the mercies of God, I urge you to present your bodies as a living sacrifice, holy and pleasing to God; this is your true worship. Do not be conformed to this age, but be transformed by the renewing of your mind, so that you may discern what is the good, pleasing, and perfect will of God.

# Mercy-Motivated Bodies

What you do with your body is based on how you view your body. Romans 12:1 tells us that our bodies are the objects of God's mercy. When you see your body in this light, you will be motivated to present your body to the God of mercy.

Here are ten statements that outline a biblical view of your bodies that is rooted in the mercy of God.

1. God created your body (Gen. 1:27). Your body is good, it is endowed with dignity, and it has a purpose.
2. Christ redeemed your body (1 Cor. 6:20). Christ purchased the right of ownership of your body when he died for you on the cross. You now belong to him.
3. The Holy Spirit indwells your body (1 Cor. 6:19). If you are a Christian, your body is now the temple of God's Spirit.
4. The Lord will raise up your body (1 Cor. 6:14). If you are dead when Christ returns, your body will be raised.

Therefore . . .

5. Give your body to God (Rom. 6:13). Decisively present each part of your body to God for his purposes and use.
6. Guide the use of your body by the power of God's Spirit and the instruction of his Word (Eph. 5:18).
7. Serve God and others with your body (Rom. 6:13).
8. Value sexual purity in your body (1 Cor. 6:13). Your sexuality is powerful and carries enormous potential for good and evil. The purity of the body is one of the greatest ways you live out your faith.
9. Value and care for your health and the health of others (Matt. 14:16).
10. Be willing to expend your energy and ultimately to lose your life to proclaim Christ and remain faithful to him (Acts 20:24). The history of Christianity is full of martyrs who understood that, while the body is good, it is not ultimate. Hold your body to be less dear to you than loyalty to our Lord Jesus Christ.

I don't know when and how you will next need to apply this view of your body to a real situation of life, but I encourage you to meditate on the mercy of God and rehearse these truths in your mind so you will be ready to obey in the moment of decision.

## ——— Philippians 3:1–11 ———

In addition, my brothers and sisters, rejoice in the
Lord. To write to you again about this is no trouble for
me and is a safeguard for you.

Watch out for the dogs, watch out for the evil
workers, watch out for those who mutilate the flesh.
For we are the circumcision, the ones who worship by
the Spirit of God, boast in Christ Jesus, and do not put
confidence in the flesh—although I have reasons for
confidence in the flesh. If anyone else thinks he has
grounds for confidence in the flesh, I have more: circumcised the eighth day; of the nation of Israel, of the
tribe of Benjamin, a Hebrew born of Hebrews; regarding the law, a Pharisee; regarding zeal, persecuting the
church; regarding the righteousness that is in the law,
blameless.

But everything that was a gain to me, I have considered to be a loss because of Christ. More than that,
I also consider everything to be a loss in view of the
surpassing value of knowing Christ Jesus my Lord.
Because of him I have suffered the loss of all things
and consider them as dung, so that I may gain Christ
and be found in him, not having a righteousness of
my own from the law, but one that is through faith in
Christ—the righteousness from God based on faith. My
goal is to know him and the power of his resurrection
and the fellowship of his sufferings, being conformed
to his death, assuming that I will somehow reach the
resurrection from among the dead.

# Loss and Gain

There is an aspect of our human nature that is rarely realized and almost never acknowledged: we all are self-righteous.

The only difference between people is the standard we use to assure ourselves that we possess some sort of rightness in this world and with God. This standard can be religious or cultural. We believe that as long as we are keeping up with the beliefs and practices of whatever religious system to which we belong, or whatever the common cultural orthodoxy of the moment is, then we are righteous.

This standard can be ethnic, racial, or national. We often think that we possess a kind of rightness based on our birth and our belonging. The important thing, as this line of thinking goes, is to belong to the right group of people. If we do, we are right.

At some point in our lives, the best thing that can happen to us is to be stripped of our sense of self-righteousness. It is a good day when we see that the standards we are using to be right with the world and God are the wrong ones, and that meeting them is inadequate.

Losing our sense of righteousness can be a great gain. Stripped of self, we have the opportunity to look to another to be clothed in true righteousness. We look up, not in. We rely on Christ, not self. We come to know assurance and joy to replace uncertainty and fear. Our restless and striving souls can finally rest and live.

The good news is that we can come to possess the righteousness that is from God through faith in Jesus Christ. This is the message of Philippians 3:1–11. I hope you will spend some time today considering Philippians 3, and the reality that righteousness cannot be earned, but can only come from God, through faith in Jesus.

# 2 Corinthians 4:8–18

We are afflicted in every way but not crushed; we are perplexed but not in despair; we are persecuted but not abandoned; we are struck down but not destroyed. We always carry the death of Jesus in our body, so that the life of Jesus may also be displayed in our body. For we who live are always being given over to death for Jesus's sake, so that Jesus's life may also be displayed in our mortal flesh. So then, death is at work in us, but life in you. And since we have the same spirit of faith in keeping with what is written, I believed, therefore I spoke, we also believe, and therefore speak. For we know that the one who raised the Lord Jesus will also raise us with Jesus and present us with you. Indeed, everything is for your benefit so that, as grace extends through more and more people, it may cause thanksgiving to increase to the glory of God.

Therefore we do not give up. Even though our outer person is being destroyed, our inner person is being renewed day by day. For our momentary light affliction is producing for us an absolutely incomparable eternal weight of glory. So we do not focus on what is seen, but on what is unseen. For what is seen is temporary, but what is unseen is eternal.

# We Do Not Give Up

The apostle Paul said, "We do not give up." Really? It seems like we are always losing heart and getting discouraged. I can think of a thousand reasons Christians would give up. Two reasons are found in 2 Corinthians 4.

We give up because of the perceived weakness of the gospel. We look around and see so much unbelief, and we look within and see so much progress to be made. We wonder if the gospel of Jesus Christ is really the message of hope and transformation for others and us.

We give up because of the obvious weakness of our humanity. We feel our human weakness and limitation and wonder if God's Spirit is really in us. With weakness like this, can we really walk with God and serve Christ? Can we really be happy?

So how can Paul say, "We do not give up"? By looking to God. In the perceived weakness of the gospel, he sees God's power to shine light in our hearts so we can see the glory of God in the face of Christ. The gospel is not weak; it is the message God uses to awaken us to Christ.

In the obvious weakness of our humanity Paul sees God's power. God uses us to contain and dispense the message of Jesus. Paul sees that while this human body is wasting away, the inner self is being renewed and we are waiting for what will be new and glorious in eternity. Our humanity is weak, but God is preparing an eternal glory for us.

You may not be tempted to give up today, but someone you know might be. Encourage that person today. Pray for them. Lift their heads and point their eyes to Jesus. If you are tempted to lose heart and give up today, believe in the power of God and his gospel, and look to him for relief.

But everything that was a gain to me, I have considered to be a loss because of Christ. More than that, I also consider everything to be a loss in view of the surpassing value of knowing Christ Jesus my Lord. Because of him I have suffered the loss of all things and consider them as dung, so that I may gain Christ and be found in him, not having a righteousness of my own from the law, but one that is through faith in Christ—the righteousness from God based on faith. My goal is to know him and the power of his resurrection and the fellowship of his sufferings, being conformed to his death, assuming that I will somehow reach the resurrection from among the dead.

Not that I have already reached the goal or am already perfect, but I make every effort to take hold of it because I also have been taken hold of by Christ Jesus. Brothers and sisters, I do not consider myself to have taken hold of it. But one thing I do: Forgetting what is behind and reaching forward to what is ahead, I pursue as my goal the prize promised by God's heavenly call in Christ Jesus. Therefore, let all of us who are mature think this way. And if you think differently about anything, God will reveal this also to you. In any case, we should live up to whatever truth we have attained.

# Your Whole Life at a Glance

If you like the big picture view of things, you will love Philippians 3. This chapter presents the whole life of a Christian, from beginning to end, in the space of a paragraph.

I must clarify: Philippians 3 will not give you the details of your life or the secret meaning to certain events of your life. You will not find a way to make decisions that will guarantee success or keep you from pain. This paragraph is not about seeing the future so you can predetermine the path of least resistance. Philippians 3 is not a crystal ball.

What we have instead is a view of life that begins with Christ, continues with him, and ends with him.

Specifically, Philippians 3:7–16 says we were made right with God to know Christ and to share in his life of death and resurrection. But, in this life, things are not perfect, and this knowledge of Christ is not complete. We don't need to be overly discouraged, however, because the end of this life for the Christian is resurrection with Christ, which will bring renewal, transformation, fullness, and completion in the knowledge of him and the experience of his life.

What about now? Our lives in Christ now are a forward progression toward knowing Christ. We press on now for what we know will be ours in the future. This is the whole life of a Christian—to come to know Christ, to continue to know him, and to fully know him someday. "To live is Christ and to die is gain" (Phil. 1:21).

I hope this passage of Scripture, which tells you about your whole life as a Christian, will encourage you today.

## Hebrews 12:1-3

Therefore, since we also have such a large cloud of witnesses surrounding us, let us lay aside every hindrance and the sin that so easily ensnares us. Let us run with endurance the race that lies before us, keeping our eyes on Jesus, the source and perfecter of our faith. For the joy that lay before him, he endured the cross, despising the shame, and sat down at the right hand of the throne of God.

For consider him who endured such hostility from sinners against himself, so that you won't grow weary and give up.

# The Need for Endurance

The last time I ran a marathon, I wanted to change the course distance at mile twenty. I wanted to exchange my lungs and legs for those of an elite athlete. I wanted to move the hands of the clock forward so the race would be over. But what I had to do instead was run with endurance.

"You need endurance," says the writer of the letter to the Hebrews in the New Testament (Heb. 10:36). The listeners who heard the letter read were a discouraged, fearful, and distracted group of people. They were tempted to cool off in their commitment to Christ or to quit and turn back from him altogether. They probably thought they needed some kind of change in their circumstances that would make the life of devotion to Christ easier. What they heard, however, was that they needed steadfast faith to continue on with Christ whether or not their circumstances ever changed.

We all need the endurance of faith. Endurance comes not by changing things or even by changing our basic personality makeup, but by looking to Jesus and keeping our gaze on him. This is the message of the letter of Hebrews.

We all need the vision of Christ and the call to endure that is in Hebrews. I pray today that you will set before yourself a vision of "him who endured such hostility from sinners against himself, so that you won't grow weary and give up."

## Philippians 1:27–30

Just one thing: As citizens of heaven, live your life worthy of the gospel of Christ. Then, whether I come and see you or am absent, I will hear about you that you are standing firm in one spirit, in one accord, contending together for the faith of the gospel, not being frightened in any way by your opponents. This is a sign of destruction for them, but of your salvation—and this is from God. For it has been granted to you on Christ's behalf not only to believe in him, but also to suffer for him, since you are engaged in the same struggle that you saw I had and now hear that I have.

# Steadfastness

Not long ago, there was a snowstorm in Nashville that reminded us of the importance of stability. A slip on the ice or a car headed into a ditch means we're off balance and out of control. That's frightening.

When it comes to our faith, we often feel unstable, as if we're on ice. We desperately need steadfastness.

Steadfastness refers to several qualities coming together into one. Steadfastness is being sure, reliable, established, and enduring. Certainly God's love is steadfast in all of these ways. Psalm 136 says, "His steadfast love endures forever" (ESV). But what about our faith? Are we standing firm?

God is the one who establishes us in the faith, making us steadfast people. Philippians 1:27–30 tells us two ways God is doing this. First, he gives us the record of his faithfulness, power, and love in the Bible. This builds our confidence in him, which in turn gives us greater stability in our faith.

Second, he gives us each other so we can strive side by side for the faith of the gospel. We help each other keep our footing as we walk by faith.

God is building steadfastness into our lives. He is building steadfastness into your life. And he is the God whose steadfast love endures forever.

## 1 Corinthians 15:20–28

But as it is, Christ has been raised from the dead, the firstfruits of those who have fallen asleep. For since death came through a man, the resurrection of the dead also comes through a man. For just as in Adam all die, so also in Christ all will be made alive.

But each in his own order: Christ, the firstfruits; afterward, at his coming, those who belong to Christ. Then comes the end, when he hands over the kingdom to God the Father, when he abolishes all rule and all authority and power. For he must reign until he puts all his enemies under his feet. The last enemy to be abolished is death. For God has put everything under his feet. Now when it says "everything" is put under him, it is obvious that he who puts everything under him is the exception. When everything is subject to Christ, then the Son himself will also be subject to the one who subjected everything to him, so that God may be all in all.

# Our Labor Will Not Be in Vain

I once visited a health clinic for women after preaching on 1 Corinthians 15 about the resurrection of the dead. While there, I heard how everyday clinic workers have conversations with women making the decision to carry or terminate the life of babies in the womb.

Throughout that week, I continued to meditate on 1 Corinthians 15 and the new bodies Christians will have in the kingdom of God, bodies fit to enjoy the goodness of the new creation and the glory of God for eternity. During the same week, a scandal broke out about abortion clinic workers who had conversations regarding how to best end a human life in the womb so as to preserve the body parts of these boys and girls for future use. My mind was swirling and my heart was grieving. They continue to do so.

On one hand, we revel in the grace of God who created and loves life and will make all things new, including our bodies, to enjoy life for eternity. On the other hand, we grieve to see utter disregard for the most basic of all human dignities: the right to life itself. I am mindful of those lives lost to the practice of abortion, and of those who have directly or indirectly participated in abortion, knowing that the toll on their conscience must be high. I'm longing for them to find a conscience-cleansing Savior in Jesus.

Many Christians have given their lives to put an end to the harmful, dignity-destroying practices of our world—from abortion to slavery to human trafficking to ethnic cleansing. We are often tempted, when we look at the state of the world today, to throw up our hands and ask, *Have any of these efforts been worth it?*

But 1 Corinthians 15 speaks a word of hope into these tragedies. Jesus said to pray, "Thy kingdom come, Thy will be done in earth as it is in heaven" (KJV). And, he said, "seek first the kingdom of God" (Matt. 6:33). This praying and seeking only makes sense if it will prove to be worth it in the end, if Christ really will bring the kingdom in its fullness to us. He will. So, as 1 Corinthians 15:58 says, "be steadfast, immovable, always excelling in the Lord's work, because you know that your labor in the Lord is not in vain."

Let us keep at the good work of proclaiming the gospel to all people so they can live forever in the kingdom of God. Let's continue our efforts to protect all human life created in the image and glory of God. And, let's keep persuading others that life lived by the values of the kingdom of God is the best life possible on earth for all people. Christ has been raised. All those who are in Christ will be raised like him. Our labor now will not be in vain.

Then Jesus left the Jordan, full of the Holy Spirit, and was led by the Spirit in the wilderness for forty days to be tempted by the devil. He ate nothing during those days, and when they were over, he was hungry. The devil said to him, "If you are the Son of God, tell this stone to become bread."

But Jesus answered him, "It is written: Man must not live on bread alone."

So he took him up and showed him all the kingdoms of the world in a moment of time. The devil said to him, "I will give you their splendor and all this authority, because it has been given over to me, and I can give it to anyone I want. If you, then, will worship me, all will be yours."

And Jesus answered him, "It is written: Worship the Lord your God, and serve him only."

So he took him to Jerusalem, had him stand on the pinnacle of the temple, and said to him, "If you are the Son of God, throw yourself down from here. For it is written: He will give his angels orders concerning you, to protect you, and they will support you with their hands, so that you will not strike your foot against a stone."

And Jesus answered him, "It is said: Do not test the Lord your God."

After the devil had finished every temptation, he departed from him for a time.

# Do the Next Right Thing

While preparing to preach from this passage a few years back, I tried to understand the nature of each temptation. What does each one mean? How does each one apply to us? It dawned on me that even though each temptation does mean something specific for Jesus and his mission, and each one does help us in our temptations, the one big lesson in the temptations of Jesus is that we are simply called to do the next right thing. Our priority should be to do what we know we are to do today, this moment, and not be distracted.

Jesus was led into the wilderness by the Holy Spirit to fast and pray, and to keep doing that until he was told by the Father to do otherwise. Jesus was not told to use his divine power to work miracles, to turn stones into bread, or to jump off buildings to prove he would not get hurt. That was the devil's idea. As far as we know, he was to simply go into the wilderness until the Spirit led him to leave the wilderness. That's what God told him to do. He couldn't listen to the devil's temptations and succumb to his distractions. He had to do the next right thing, the thing the Father told him to do.

In Jesus, we see that obedience to God in the next thing is always the right way. It may not be easy, but neither is it complicated. There are many distractions, but the calling is clear. Do the next right thing.

Don't complicate obedience to God. What's the next right thing for you to do? Is it to love your spouse? To go to work? To pay a bill? To kill a thought? To break off a relationship? To read a book? To help a neighbor? To say, "I love you"? To apologize? Forgive? Volunteer? Give? Pray? Sleep? What is it that you know you need to do now?

Don't get distracted. Keep doing the next right thing, today, for forty days, and for the rest of your life. You have no idea what the future holds, and you certainly can't control it. So take today, and in obedience to God, being led by the Holy Spirit, do the next right thing.

## PHILIPPIANS 1:21–26

For me, to live is Christ and to die is gain. Now if I live on in the flesh, this means fruitful work for me; and I don't know which one I should choose. I am torn between the two. I long to depart and be with Christ—which is far better—but to remain in the flesh is more necessary for your sake. Since I am persuaded of this, I know that I will remain and continue with all of you for your progress and joy in the faith, so that, because of my coming to you again, your boasting in Christ Jesus may abound.

# Life and Death

There was a time when the sermons, songs, and conversations of the church reflected the Bible's priority on life and death and on life in relation to death. It seems we have gotten away from this priority and shifted to themes more related to life only and to life disconnected from death.

I suspect one reason for this shift is our desire to figure out how Christianity relates to our present experiences with family, career, and the things of this world. But the problem with separating life and death in our thinking and deemphasizing the gospel perspective on death altogether is that we cannot know how to live now unless we understand what life will hold after we die.

The apostle Paul said, "For me, to live is Christ and to die is gain" (Phil. 1:21). Paul is keeping life and death together in his thinking. He understands that the gospel speaks to both, and that the two are related. The gospel is the good news of Christ, and Christ shapes the way we live now, and determines our experience of life after we die. We can also say that the gospel tells us what life after we die will be like, so it shapes how we live now.

Life and death are opportunities to honor Christ because in each one people "in Christ" experience his grace. In life, we experience the lordship of Christ over us as forgiven and reconciled people. In death, we experience the lordship of Christ in a fuller measure that is described as "gain." This is because when we die as Christians we will see Christ without the cloudiness of this life, we will know Christ without the partialness of this life, and we will be like Christ without the immaturity of this life. We will see him clearly, know him fully, and be like him maturely.

Since that is what life after we die will be, that is what life now is becoming. We are called now to seek Christ, grow in knowledge of Christ, and conform our lives to the life of Christ.

Think today about life and death and how both relate to the good news of Jesus Christ. Spend a few minutes making some observations from this passage about God, yourself, life, and death. Talk to someone about this passage and your observations. Pray for your church and the other churches in your city, that they will preach the fullness of the gospel in its relation to life and death.

## Hebrews 13:7–16

Remember your leaders who have spoken God's word to you. As you carefully observe the outcome of their lives, imitate their faith. Jesus Christ is the same yesterday, today, and forever. Don't be led astray by various kinds of strange teachings; for it is good for the heart to be established by grace and not by food regulations, since those who observe them have not benefited. We have an altar from which those who worship at the tabernacle do not have a right to eat. For the bodies of those animals whose blood is brought into the most holy place by the high priest as a sin offering are burned outside the camp. Therefore, Jesus also suffered outside the gate, so that he might sanctify the people by his own blood. Let us then go to him outside the camp, bearing his disgrace. For we do not have an enduring city here; instead, we seek the one to come. Therefore, through him let us continually offer up to God a sacrifice of praise, that is, the fruit of lips that confess his name. Don't neglect to do what is good and to share, for God is pleased with such sacrifices.

# Stay with Jesus

Hebrews 13:8 says, "Jesus Christ is the same yesterday, today, and forever." The verses that follow in Hebrews 13 tell us that since Jesus remains the same, we are to remain with him. Here at the close of Hebrews, the message of endurance is given again: stay with Jesus.

Stay with the cross of Jesus as your truth. Staying with Jesus means not being led away from the cross by teachings about other means of salvation.

Stay with the name of Jesus in your worship. We are to continually say "thank you" to God through Jesus and for Jesus.

Stay with the example of Jesus in your living. We follow Jesus by doing good.

Think about Hebrews 13:7–16 today, and ask yourself these questions: Am I holding on to the truth of the cross and trusting in the cross? Am I continually giving praise to God for Jesus? Today, in tasks, conversations, and decisions, am I following Jesus as a servant to others?

Staying with Jesus is enduring in truth, worship, and obedience. Think on these things.

# Conclusion

For one hundred days you have read the Bible, along with a few comments from me. I have tried to explain the Bible passages and show some application of them to your life. I hope you have gained a greater desire to read the Bible each day, and to think about its place in your life.

I also hope that you have found a method for your daily time of reading God's Word. You can read the Bible without a companion book. You can even write your own companion book. The *Words of Grace* devotional book is simply a collection of my thoughts on God's Word that I wanted my congregation to read. But even if these devotionals were never read by others, the process of reading, reflecting, praying, and writing would still have benefited me.

Each day as you read the Bible, write your thoughts and prayers. You will be amazed at how deeply you will engage with God and his words of grace. Your writings may not become a book, but your faith will be strengthened by this process. You will also have something to share with others. In private conversations with people who need to know God's grace in Christ, or in a small group of people who are trying to grow in their faith, you can share your own thoughts about God's Word.

Interacting with God's Word in prayer, deep thought, and journaling will help you and others know God and follow his Son, Jesus, by grace through faith. So, keep going. Let day 101 be the day you write your own *Words of Grace*.

# Acknowledgments

Grace Community Church of Nashville is the congregation where I have been a member, elder, and pastor for twenty-five years. Thank you, my dear friends, for helping me be a better follower of Jesus, for encouraging me to be a faithful pastor and preacher, and for loving God's words of grace. Thank you for "showing up."

Nanette Ryan and Sondra Jackson have faithfully served Grace Community Church and have proofed and edited every *Words of Grace* devotional before they were sent to our congregation and posted online. Thank you for "cleaning me up."

Jay and Kristi Smith, friends and fellow church members, used their creative abilities for the design of this book. Thank you for adding your artistic touch to the printed word.

The team at B&H Publishing (Jennifer Lyell, Taylor Combs, Devin Maddox, and Scott Corbin) have been so helpful and encouraging in the publication of this book. Thank you for guiding me through the process.

My wife, Beth, reads every *Words of Grace* devotional before anyone else. Her honest feedback has helped me keep the message clear. Thank you, my love, for being my partner in life.